HOW TO MANIFEST YOUR **BEST DAMN LIFE** THROUGH **YOU**

THE BEST OF
YOURSELF

KATHLEEN CAMERON

THE BEST OF
YOURSELF

HOW TO MANIFEST YOUR BEST DAMN LIFE THROUGH YOU

KATHLEEN CAMERON

Cover and Design Elements by Shawna Poliziani

Graphics Created by Diamond Academy Coaching Inc

Editing by Nancy Haight

ISBN: 978-1-7380987-0-5 (hardcover)
ISBN: 978-1-7380987-2-9 (softcover)
ISBN: 978-1-7380987-1-2 (ebook)

Book Design by HMDpublishing

Produced in Collaboration with Live Your Dreams Out Loud Inc

CONTENTS

ENDORSEMENTS

For me, Kathleen was a complete game-changer. Before I met Kathleen, I had tried so many other things, had various coaches, and took a lot of courses, but nothing compared to what Kathleen teaches and how she teaches. Since coaching with Kathleen, I've 10 x'd my business, found my soulmate, and become an author and a speaker. She showed me just how much power within I have and how to use it.

With gratitude,
Holly Carroll
Luxury Realtor, Author, Public Speaker, and former Miss Canada

Kathleen Cameron is the epitome of inspiration. The work that she has done to be the best version of herself is a testament to what's possible. Since I've met her, I've learned more about myself, the possibilities, and what's at stake for my life if I just do the work. I'm grateful for her humanness, her business, and the lives that she impacts daily. The world is better because of her commitment to be the best of herself.

Brian D. Johnson
Bestselling Author and Founder of Live Your Dreams Out Loud Inc.

The Best Of Yourself guides you step by step on your quest to manifest the life you want and deserve, building a foundation first within yourself, then others, and finally the world!

Remember that your thoughts are powerful and that thoughts become things. With that being said, this will be the most valuable book you read this year.

Michael Collins
Founder and CEO of Triiiangle

Kathleen Cameron is a must-read. She is a woman whose chosen path has positively impacted so many individuals you will want to share this material with your life who will benefit.

Judy O'Leary
Bestselling author of *Twigs Christmas Adventure*, and community volunteer.

Kathleen Cameron is the embodiment of inspiration. Her journey to self-improvement is a living example of potential realized. Through our acquaintance, I've unearthed insights into my own self and the achievable prospects, understanding the significance of dedicated efforts in shaping my life's trajectory. With appreciation for her authenticity, business acumen, and daily life influence, Kathleen elevates our world through her unwavering pursuit of personal excellence.

Ana Raynes
CEO and Founder of Simplified Impact

Kathleen has profoundly impacted my life since the first day I met her. Her genuine passion and positive nature leave a lasting impression. She has taught me to love, lead, and serve with authenticity, always being true to who I am from within.

Kathleen teaches consistently with utmost simplicity and a heart of gold. My deepest desire has been manifested to be taught and transformed by a mentor who embodies and lives by giving, living, and thriving as the best of herself. I am forever grateful and transformed.

Debora Gattola
Top Success Advisor for Diamond Academy

Kathleen is the ORACLE, the mother of manifestation, and attracts the best and highest into one's life. She has a heart of gold and a spirit of supernatural knowledge. She is what she teaches and preaches. She's the true embodiment of her work!

Eric Bigger
Personal Development Coach & TV Personality

Kathleen is a visionary paving the way for others to create the love and life they desire—a living testament to the transformative power of manifestation and possibility.

Jon Talarico
Founder of The Million in You

Kathleen Cameron is a gifted teacher, thought leader, and modern mentor who takes you on a path of self-awareness, self-love, and self-concept to become the best of yourself.

Immersing in her energy and embodying her teachings can and will change your life.

Choose to study her work, and let yourself be open to being your divine version and creating an extraordinary life. You are only one decision away…..

Jennifer Underwood
Gratitude & Abundance Coach; # 1 Bestselling Author

Through Kathleen's guidance, I've learned to rewrite my story, manifest my dreams, and tap into a wellspring of potential I never knew existed. This book is not just a collection of ideas; it's a portal to a reality where success and fulfillment are within reach. It's a testament to Kathleen's dedication to helping others achieve their true potential and become the architects of their destiny.

Kacie Tilker

Kathleen's presence when she speaks and when you read the Best of Yourself invites you to see your best self, your highest self…and what's blocking that version from showing up. I love how she guides you to shift into a beautiful flow of becoming the best of yourself instead of a relentless striving that leaves you exhausted.

The Best of Yourself will be a modern classic that lovingly invites your best to come out and play…If you want to show up as beautifully and powerfully as you are, the Best of Yourself is a MUST-read!

Mike Zeller

By looking into Kathleen's eyes, you know she has tapped into something extraordinary, and she not only used it to embody her best self, but she now shares with the world how we can all do it, too. Knowing Kathleen has transformed my life in endless wonderful ways, including the growth of HUMANHOOD. If you can receive any of her wisdom through her words, presence, or programs, fully embrace it, it will change your life! The Best of Yourself will shake you to the core and awaken your power to create your best life.

Julia Robert
HUMANHOOD co-founder

ACKNOWLEDGMENTS

I would not be writing this book if it wasn't for Mr. Bob Proctor. To say this man changed my life is an understatement. I remember on a live event with him, I once said, "Anything for Bob," and that's absolutely how I continue to live my life to this day. He dedicated his life to helping people access their greatest potential, and I am here to continue what he started so generously.

To my family. You have been everything to me. I cannot be who I am today and spend the time on this book without your support. I am so grateful to be surrounded by the most loving, caring, and supportive people I know. Mom, Dad, Carly, Chris and Chris Cameron, I love you all deeply. You mean more to me than I can express.

To my Diamond Academy family, my team, and my students, my growth has been through your growth. If it wasn't for your trust, your devotion, and your willingness to expand your own awareness, I would not be who I am today.

And to you, the reader. I acknowledge you for your bravery, for your desire for more, and for your boldness in going after it. Once you realize you make a significant impact on this world, just by thinking in a new way, you will have a new-found passion and zest for life. You are important and you are bettering this world by becoming the best of yourself.

To our combined impact,

Kathleen

DEDICATION

To my girls, Masyn and Raegan.
Everything I do is for you.

INTRODUCTION

The light that is my life today is not the same light I knew before. As little as 3.5 years ago, there were endless days, weeks, and months of darkness, cloudiness, blindness, and confusion. The light (or lack thereof) was different, or perhaps it was the perception through my own eyes that was not the same. It felt like I was floating up and above my own life, watching myself hit the same walls repeatedly, unable to locate the next step towards a more fulfilling life. I was repeatedly wanting more, circling myself over and over again, and ending up in the same place. My life was a constant rinse and repeat of the same routine over and over again. I would ask myself, Is this really what life is all about?

Have you woken up today in your very own version of Groundhog Day? Has the mentality of living day by day begun to wear on your heart and soul? Perhaps you're consumed by negative thoughts, self-destructive patterns, unhealthy habits, or a general lack of self-care. It could be that you feel lost or hopeless.

Even if you are going through the motions, your discontent has continued to rise. You've considered the poor decision making, the circumstances of your family, the indecisiveness in your past. You might be lying in bed at night worrying about finances or your kid's education or how you'll afford an emergency if, God forbid, one were to occur. Would you be curious if I said I have been there too?

Unsurprisingly, the source of your lingering pain can be difficult to pinpoint, especially when there are a variety of causes. I like to think of this reality as similar to the simulated world in *The Matrix*—that mundane monotony where we can't seem to see how what we want is actually attainable. We see others living these lives of freedom, and we think to ourselves, *I wish that were me!* We all know that life happens, and like the past version of me, you may believe it is happening to you and around you. You go through the rhythms of life, without direction, while the question still presses against your mind: *Is this really all there is?* I am here as living proof that there is far more, and it happens through YOU, not to you.

So, while you desperately want some grand change, you don't have the means to make it happen. You've become stuck in this deep rut, but you haven't considered the escape route. How could you even fathom one when life does its best to keep you down?

When I was a young girl, I felt that I simply wasn't good enough. This continued for years and years. Truthfully, what I wanted was to be like someone else. I spent decades wishing that I looked different. I spent years wishing that I was different. I longed to be more beautiful, more active, more confident, more agreeable, funnier, wittier, wiser. Who I was simply was not enough.

This feeling lingered well into adulthood. While I felt content from time to time, I wouldn't say I was satisfied with the state of my life. I lacked self-worth, and my negativity spread outward. Others struggled to see the good in me because I could barely see it in myself. Many of my actions stemmed from never feeling like I was enough. I was persistently distracted from seeing myself in a healthy way.

This distraction broke when I reached 37 years of age. I realized there had to be more the world had to offer and that something within my reality needed to change. I was tired of living a life that was entirely made of orchestrated versions of me other people desired to see and never the version of me that I desired to be.

Of course, I had some ideas of what my change would look like. In fact, most people have a vivid image of their "perfect" self; cemented in their head is an idea of who they'd like to be. Mine involved the word *skinny*. The perfect Kathleen was thin, and I never saw it any other way. When I was thin, I would be accepted. When I considered my self-image—a term I no longer use often—I ruminated on adding a shift in attitude, a new wardrobe, perfecting my posture. For others, it might be a new career, a new house, a new body. Whatever it is, when you've deeply longed for it, eventually it becomes unbearable to ignore.

I started to imagine a new, improved Kathleen. Before I knew it, this 'perfect' concept of myself became the vision of who I was from the outside in, not the inside out. I found myself taking other people's suggestions more seriously than my own self-reflection. Some of these suggestions were in bad faith, but I just didn't know it yet.

Throwing myself into this change, I began to believe that the clearest path to my best self was weight loss. I kept track of carbs, calories, and macros. I exercised regularly and increasingly, chugged liters of water every day, and monitored my sleep. I did everything I could do to keep the weight off. I lost 100 pounds two different times, and every time I gained the weight back, I could feel the judgments come with it.

In 2018, after losing over 100 pounds in eleven months, my health was becoming dangerously shaky. I began to have fainting spells. They became so frequent that I could barely make it to the grocery store. My strict diet was not only dangerous, but it was also psychologically debilitating. The mentality I held was eating me alive instead. On the outside, I looked healthy. The image I portrayed to the world was one of confidence, happiness, and strength, but on the inside, it was a different story. I was thin but unhealthy.

It's safe to say that I was hardly building the best version of myself. In contrast, I was creating someone new in their image. One day in 2019, I woke up and I felt like a stranger to my own self. I barely recognized myself or the person I'd become. This new me had nothing to do with the real me. I thought my weight loss would lead to a better life with an improved self image, more money, and more success. It alternatively led to an unhealthy lifestyle and a rejection of my authentic self, which was emotionally damaging. Something had to give.

After all this effort, my life still felt stagnant. At times, it even felt like I was moving backwards. I hoped for a path to better myself and started putting in the work. In September of that year, a leader in my business mentioned she had hired a coach, and I thought maybe I should do the same. Not a week later, I was introduced to Bob Proctor and signed up for one of his programs to help grow my business. This was a few months after I had left my nursing career after an extended sick leave. His help as my teacher and mentor ended up changing the trajectory of my life and led me to establishing my own mentorship program.

Despite my past of being the fly running incessantly into the window, I had finally reached my own beautiful door out into the luminous world. The pathway to a joyous life filled with fulfillment and luxury was made clear. Now I not only live as my best self, but I also coach clients in doing the same. Life is beautiful, and I feel it. The best part? I am me—the real me. There is no greater freedom.

My first book, *Becoming the One,* detailed my path toward finally deciding to create the life I wanted—my extraordinary life. It focused on the launch of my coaching career and how this success manifested so quickly. While it explained the "what" and the "why," it didn't involve much teaching or the "how" so many long for. The story of my initial quantum leap gave many people a roadmap toward their own awakening; however, so much was left to the imagination. My goal in the first book was to tell my story, not to fluff it up. I kept it simple and light.

With this in mind, my goal with *The Best of Yourself* is to take my personal transformation into becoming the best version of myself and to present it as a "how-to" for others. I want to deliver messages that not only resonate with others but also form the framework for their own transformations.

Throughout the book, I will present actionable steps as well as my philosophy behind building self-esteem and personal development. Beyond my teaching, I will present stories from either my life or a client who has studied under me and applied these concepts. My ultimate hope is that these anecdotes will illuminate the concepts we explore. Each chapter will end with a journal prompt so you can actively practice the teachings and transfer the knowledge to your own life.

In our journey together, you will leave with something tangible and attainable. At this point, you may be wondering: *Who exactly is this book for? How can it help me?*

This book is for those who desire to become the best version of themselves. This won't teach you how to compete with others or feel superior. Instead, it will help you to harness the beauty that lies buried within and to bring it to the surface, while collaborating with others beautifully. It's not about becoming a new and improved version of you that you have never been. It's about becoming aware of versions of you that already exist deep within.

Ultimately, it will show what you are capable of, highlighting how your unique strengths set you apart from others, and illustrate just how much you are able to accomplish in this world. It is about activating the best possible timeline of your life and inviting in the blessings that being you can bring.

This all begins with the decision to understand yourself. It cannot happen any other way than by curiosity, awareness, and love. Once this belief in yourself is established, you can translate it to success. Of course, what it means to be successful differs from person to person.

Despite this, our definition of success still stems from the same source—a desire for wholeness, fulfillment, happiness, peace, ease, flow, authenticity, love, and calmness. These ideals serve as stepping stones on one's quest to escape that murky, mundane world of *The Matrix*. Let this remind you of your potential and your ability to shift your circumstances.

We are all naturally in a state of growth. Whether we like it or not, we are actively expanding. This is the way in which we exist—in energy, in spirit, and in physical experience —on this plane. The problem is that we've been taught to stop this expansion. We're often told to stop our growth, even when it is the natural state of being. If we take this command seriously, our life circumstances start to resemble *Groundhog Day*. We cease to be dreamers, even though dreamers are the ones changing the world.

My mentor Bob Proctor used to say, "We are either expanding or disintegrating," and this book is for anyone wishing to break the cycle of disintegration and to continue expanding and ascending into the best of themselves while impacting the world in a positive way.

While my words are for everyone, I understand that I am deeply connected to a certain type of individual who is driven, hardworking, and a selfless caregiver who does more for others than for themselves. I imagine they want more out of this life but don't see that as a possibility. This is because I have been that person before.

I've met so many who are stuck in this state. They are unfulfilled, overworked, and feel unworthy. I can empathize with this situation. I've felt the displeasure and disintegration caused by pursuing the wrong life. With my whole being, I am reaching out to this individual and telling them that there's more—it comes down to asking the right questions and making the right choices.

In the modern world, personal growth and development are becoming a normal part of life. They are not just for people seeking self-help. Many are dissatisfied with their current script and are willing to change. They seek guidance, as each of us do in our uniqueness.

Ultimately, *The Best of Yourself* is a roadmap for creating a life that makes you truly proud and enthusiastic to be who you really are. It's about investing in yourself and growing through your spirit. It focuses on transforming your perspective of yourself, which in turn helps you transform your whole life for the better. It's where spirituality meets personal growth and development— being present in the NOW while expanding who you are for what's next.

On your journey to becoming your best, I will serve as messenger and teacher, injecting my understanding of the divine with a critical perspective pulled from my personal experience. The insights I have are intended to raise your consciousness so you can also awaken your spirit, mind, and body in preparation for profound change. By affecting each individual, I hope to raise the collective consciousness, one mind at a time.

I won't pretend I have all the answers. Even if I did, I respect your individuality and how you interpret my words. I only hope my ideas illuminate your personal journey and that you find comfort and wisdom in my words as you forge ahead. This book should engage your critical thinking reflexes so you can look inward and question your own routines and beliefs:

What do I believe about life and about myself?

Why do I believe this?

What do I easily accept? What do I reject?

As you begin the journey inward, we often find the part we each play in our own displeasure. You may come to see what is directly caused by your own consciousness, your own outlook, your own framework that you've passively accepted. For much of my life, I believed I was in the passenger seat, waiting to see what life had to offer me. But now, I have taken the wheel; I am the driver. You'll be amazed by how much your life can change when you decide you are worthy of the best life has to offer.

As you embark on this journey to uncover the best of yourself that lies within, I would encourage you to do so with love, a curiosity to uncover your truth, and a purpose to add positivity to this world. A wonderful adventure of self-discovery awaits.

CHAPTER **ONE:**

Meeting the "Best" of Yourself

"If you want the best the world has to offer, offer the world your best."
Neale Donald Walsch

When I say BEST, I don't mean better.

"Better" and "should" slowly creep together. *I should look this way. I should exercise. I should do better in my business. I should, I should, I should.* And so we "should" ourselves into a better version of ourselves just because we think and believe that we should. The should implies a problem needing solving and a drive to grow and expand because who we are today just doesn't cut it.

So what would truly be the best of yourself? Remember, you are both the meeting and the introduction. We see what we are looking for. Now is the time to ask yourself, *what is my soul seeking?*

When you read the words "best of yourself," what immediately comes to mind? Perhaps you picture yourself impeccably dressed, charming a crowd at a dinner party, financially secure, and surrounded by family and friends. How current or distant is this imagined life from the one you're living right now? Do you picture yourself becoming this person, or is it only wishful thinking?

Most people miss this, but our idea of who we are sets up our individual experience and the way we choose to live. It drives both how we define ourselves and the energy we share with others. If you lack security or a healthy sense of self-worth, it's easy to visualize the person you'd rather be. You might consider this new, "improved" image as just outside of your reach, as if it's some elusive "you" that will never exist in the outside world, so it stays buried.

Some call this improved version of you your "higher self." I prefer not to use this language because it can be misleading. It's not necessarily about building higher; it's about digging deeper. I also refrain from using this language because who you are today is not less than or inferior—you likely just believe it is.

We oftentimes don't realize it, yet countless people reform themselves based on a false image, believing it's their "higher self." They don't realize it's an illusion. When their transformation is done, they look at themselves and hardly recognize the stranger in the mirror. They did not grow into the best of themselves. Instead, they became someone else's idea of who they are. Then they wonder why they still lack the confidence they long for.

Imagine you are presenting an art piece. Every single person that views it may share their opinion. Some comments may be helpful, and some may be hurtful. If you took every note that group gave you and recreated the artwork, what would it become? A chaotic piece only curated to please others, but never quite original and not an honest expression of the artist.

When you give into pressure and other people's perspectives, you build a faulty foundation and set yourself up for failure.

Needless to say, but necessary to admit, this was the version of my life once lived. Pleasing others did not bring me clarity or joy, but who I became from it was not someone I needed to completely discard. At that time, it wasn't necessarily about creating a new me; it was about finding what was hidden inside and harnessing it. This was the crucial moment I began to discover that you manifest what you <u>are</u>, not what you <u>want</u>.

Becoming the best version of you does not require you to leave previous parts of you behind. In fact, to put it plainly, your best simply means being better than who you were yesterday. It's not about measuring your progress against others. The goal is never to become superior to others. The past selves we were and the people around us will never be inferior either. This journey is self-expression on <u>your own terms</u>. The only comparison that's real is the one between you and you.

So how do you find what is best on your own terms? It all starts with looking inward and aligning with your authentic self. Once you discover the version of you that you're most proud of, you'll experience ultimate peace of mind with the life that you are presented with. First, you must believe that they exist already.

We have all heard the advice, "Fake it till you make it." Perhaps it was suggested to "act as if" or "be it to become it." I would instead say there's no pretending because what you desire to be or have already exists. There is no new self to strive for. It's about remembering who you really are and becoming what you now remember being. What I believe is that you have access to everything already—you are simply unaware of it. We are talking about a return to who you have always been.

Let's be transparent with one another here: what you're seeking is the truth. It moves beyond the concept of self that has been programmed in you and beyond the identity you present to other people. It rejects social conditioning and programming. Essentially, it is the realest you without any outside influence telling you how to act, how to think, how to dress, or how to be. You shed the pressure to perform for other people and replace it with your truest essence. Once you tap into what already exists, all you have to do is amplify it.

Ultimately, we can all benefit from reprogramming our mind and refocusing our identity in order to live out a different and more fulfilling experience. This isn't an entirely intellectual process. It also involves the spiritual and the physical. Without having everything in alignment, it's hard to make real progress.

Of course, this reprogramming is easier said than done. You have to fight against years of cultural pressure and negative self-talk to see yourself in an entirely different light. These obstacles can often feel impossible to overcome. Trust me when I say I've been there!

I've struggled against these influences as well. For the majority of my life, I bought into other people's ideas of what I should be. When deciding a career path, I remember all the reasons nursing would be a great career: it is a well-paid position, the profession is always needed in society, and there are many ways to succeed as a nurse. Choosing a traditional 9 to 5 career path working for someone else felt natural, because that's just what you do!

I never fully considered if I actually wanted to nurse people back to health at the bedside, be their support in their sickest moments, and face being next to someone taking their last breath. While I was honored to do so, it did not bring me joy. Saying this out loud is so freeing. Working in a field amongst heroes was rewarding, but did it bring me joy? No it did not. It was actually quite stressful and exhausting. Helping people always makes me feel like I am making a difference, but I've learned there is a way to do so that is in alignment with the real me. This version of me today is thriving because I help people in a way that brings me JOY.

Inevitably, I would reach a breaking point to escape this cycle and discover wholeness. This began with a seed of doubt where I questioned the life I'd built. From there, I began to redefine myself. After some serious introspection, I built a new idea of my personal successes, leading me to become and live my best self.

While this sounds daunting, the process I have cultivated is largely effortless. Again, it's not about creating a new self-image and reprogramming your subconscious mind over months and months. It's about amplifying your authentic self, enacting who you *really* are, and bringing the real you to the surface.

Creation and expression happens from top to bottom. It begins with the spirit, expands to the mind, and moves to the physical. This all begins with igniting your self-awareness. You might have heard of others "manifesting" with scripts, affirmations, rituals, crystals, and oracle cards, but I am here to share with you that if you desire deeply profound and lasting change, then the essential process to follow is a journey of self-discovery. Once you change the YOU you see yourself to be, these tools can be a great adjunct, but growth is the key.

I have developed my very own Four-Step Manifestation Process, one that differs from most that begin with the vision or goal to be manifested. I believe one cannot create an image of the life they truly desire until they know themselves first. The four steps begin with self awareness, move to being in spirit, followed by the regulation of the mind, and ending in the physical world with your action.

STEP ONE: Self-Awareness

Learning how to look within is the epitome to becoming your best self. As your awareness alters, the things around you change. This perspective change is often immediate, and you notice the beauty, the joy, and the love that already exists around you. While we are in a three-dimensional world, the effect ripples out to your physical observations. Suddenly, there is more money, healthier relationships, better business opportunities, a new job, and nicer people. Everything starts to work itself out with ease, because you began the work within first.

Life itself is about our awareness of it. So ultimately, manifestation involves becoming more thoroughly aware. First and foremost, you must <u>want</u> to be self-aware. There has to be some driving force within you. This often involves overcoming fears and anxieties that exist in your head and jumping into spirit. Then, you can examine who you really are and what you're worth. You start to dissect your self-concept and the energy you present.

Becoming self-aware begins with observing yourself—your thoughts, your feelings and your actions—and being introspective and asking yourself questions, not those around you.

STEP TWO: Spirit

The next important step in this journey of creating your dream life is to become aligned with the source of it all, the life force within. My first book highlighted my journey to becoming "one" with god/source/creator/ universe. I use inclusive language for the benefit of the reader; however, I use the word *God* in my own life. Choose what resonates with you. It's the god of your understanding that matters most. Whatever your beliefs, the important thing here is to tap into the creative energy all around and through you. Every one of us here is involved in its existence. Spirit is beyond the physical manifestations because it is the root of them. When we invoke our faith, directing our beliefs to focus on the core elements of our best self, then the magic begins to manifest. Ultimately, it is the belief in something outside of ourselves, a higher power, one that supports, responds, fulfills, and guides us.

STEP THREE: Intellect

The intellectual plane involves your mind and its beliefs. It is where your identity is stored. Do you know which morals you adhere to? Which behaviors and ideals would you like to change? When we are here, new ideas can emerge. The best of yourself is molded and given meaning. What most people are unaware of in this particular aspect is that our subconscious is controlling the scene. If and when we are bypassing what lies deeper in our minds—the patterns, the habits, the recurring worries, our beliefs—then they remain stuck here. All we believe, consent to, assume to be true, and act on is our consciousness, and it's this consciousness that we express through. We are who we believe ourselves to be.

STEP FOUR: Being/The Physical (Body)

The body is the space you take up in this three-dimensional realm (and what you choose to do with it). It means seizing the ideas you've built and taking intuitive action. You finally get to see reality transform to match your ideals. Here, your dreams become concrete and tangible. It is all about seeing your actions align with your new mentality. It is the vessel we have here in this physical world. Our body is capable of amplifying what our spirit is aligned with expressing. Through the lens of who our human is, we build our unique physical reality. I call this final step "embodiment".

Whenever people tell me they want to be successful, I try to dig a little deeper and imagine the desires that exist behind this. Sure, they may want a fulfilling job, financial security, and a loving family, but what they really want is wholeness, ease, flow, peace, and love. These wants are hard to articulate beyond saying we simply want the best for ourselves. So how do we make these desires tangible? How do we translate them to success? What do we need to change in order to make this happen?

Start by defining yourself. First, simply state the facts and get down to basics. For example, it could be physical features or the roles you play in life: I have brown hair. I have hazel eyes. I am a teacher. Remind yourself of what you are familiar.

Here is the tricky part: as you consider these traits, avoid ideas that other people have and use to define you. These external voices can often blur our true sense of self. Only focus on how you see yourself. Be as clear as possible. This honest internal dialogue will bring you closer to the "you" that's buried. You may find you identify in a certain way then later realize this label was never yours but one you took on from someone else. Notice the descriptors: *I'm a procrastinator, an early riser, lazy, driven,* etc.

Now we can begin to expand from there. What skills do you have? How do these skills make you exceptional, functional, unique, connected? Would you be your authentic self without them?

Next, think about how often you exercise the skills or characteristics that make you feel exhilarated in your daily life. Do any of these skills play a part in your work? Your hobbies? Your family life? You might find that you haven't exercised a skill in years or have a former obsession that you've abandoned. Tap into the passions you have and the characteristics you admire.

YOU, *yourself*, AS YOU WERE *made*, ARE *complete*.

We have all seen it time and again. When someone chooses to not fulfill their potential, their review at the end is typically grim. So we must do our part to honor the life we've been given. We do this by first moving toward a deeper self-awareness. You are now beginning to know and recognize the parts of yourself you've neglected. The next step is to find ways to align more with it. Because the truth is this: You, yourself, as you were made, are complete.

Life-changing reflections and self-awareness takes practice and patience. After all, you have grown accustomed to living an inauthentic life, so it can be a massive challenge to reframe the way you see yourself. It can also be painful to be reminded of untapped potential or unique aspects of yourself that you've pushed aside.

I am here to remind you that it is important to keep your eyes on the outcome as you question your worth, your value, and your purpose. Once you find your authentic self and exercise it, your whole life will be created by you and for you. While this newfound power can be frightening, it is freeing. The goal is never to become a new version of you, never to take on qualities of others that we believe are admirable, but to connect with and amplify the essence of ourselves. The end is the realization of who you REALLY are.

Are you ready and willing to know the best of yourself?

THE *end* IS
THE
realization
OF WHO *you*
REALLY ARE.

CHAPTER 1:
Journal Prompts

Reflect on your journey of personal growth: What are some specific ways in which you have grown and improved as an individual compared to who you were yesterday? How have these changes positively impacted your life and relationships?

Explore your self-acceptance: How do you perceive the idea of embracing all parts of yourself, including your past and present? Are there any aspects of yourself that you struggle to accept or to integrate into your journey of becoming the best version of yourself? What steps can you take to cultivate self-compassion and acceptance?

Set goals for continuous self-improvement: Based on the understanding that becoming the best version of yourself is a lifelong process, what realistic and achievable goals can you set for your personal growth? How can you incorporate these goals into your daily routine or practice? Reflect on the potential obstacles and strategies to overcome them as you strive for consistent progress.

CHAPTER **TWO:**

It's not your body being bigger that makes you flawed; it's your belief that you are that does.

This is something I have told myself time and time again, to remind me that the truth lies in my belief system.

What we believe to be true will always be our truth.

You fell for it. You believed what "they" wanted you to believe. I did too.

You aren't flawed.

You are amazing.

You are loved.

You have infinite potential.

Drop the story and return to the truth.

Your appearance has nothing to do with who you are or how much you are worth. Beauty isn't about appearance; it's about energy. The most beautiful people don't have six-pack abs and clear skin; they have a good heart. When I realized that I am not my body but I am IN my body, everything changed.

Thin does not equal success unless we believe that truth. You see my beauty because I see my beauty.

The most freeing thing I ever did was stop trying to meet a beauty ideal. We don't need to be smoothed out or snatched in. Don't minimize yourself for others. As I continue my journey of health and longevity, I keep how I look as my lowest priority on purpose.

My favorite mantra:

I AM BEAUTIFUL NOW.

The universe/God/creator responds only to how YOU feel about YOU. It does not give more to those who are smarter, thinner, sexier, or richer.

It gives more to those who believe they are worth it, to those who are grateful, to those who are confident, and to those who dare to ask for more.

I use this example because it was the biggest shift in belief that I made in my journey that led me to where I am today. For you, it could be your level of education, where you came from, your gender identity, how much money you do or don't have, your race, or your age.

What is the flaw you see in yourself that is actually your superpower?

Perceive it differently and change the reality you exist in today.

(Excerpt taken from my Social Media)

Loving yourself is the first step to becoming your best. Without self-love, the lessons in this book cannot be learned—it's as simple as that.

I know how hard the initial steps toward self-love can be, especially when that voice in your head has been putting you down for years. I didn't practice self-love prior to September 2019. I hated so many aspects of myself that it made me feel sick. There was so much I wanted to change, yet I felt hopeless in the face of my perceived flaws. I felt like I was being dragged down by my own insecurities into a never-ending spiral of negativity.

Before I developed self-love, I thought love was something that you only offered another person, not yourself. I figured it was a selfless act to turn your love outward without saving any for yourself. In contrast, I thought it must be self-centered to hold yourself in high regard. Because I didn't value myself, those who had enough confidence to value themselves felt to me like their "ego" was on overdrive. I couldn't understand or relate to it. I had no concept of what a healthy confidence looked like because I couldn't own being me and didn't feel comfortable in my skin. I struggled to find a kind word to say when I looked in the mirror. My comfort zone was unfortunately self-deprecation.

While it's often an individual struggle, this self-degrading attitude doesn't just affect you. It affects everyone in your orbit. You can't be devoid of self-love and expect others to still love you. Think about it this way: If you dislike yourself and feel you're unworthy of love, what does that say about your friends and family who love you? By your own logic, it must mean they're also unworthy of love. After all, they choose to spend their time with you. If you believe you're worth so little, why would they want to stick around? And let's think about attraction for a moment. We attract who we are, and we influence others to remain that way. So we end up in relationships with others who have no self-worth, and we keep each other right where we found each other. And even more profound, we teach our children, our nieces and nephews, and our grandkids how easy it is to be self-critical, fearful, and judgmental. This perspective of self is learned, and we are teaching it by being it.

THIS *perspective* OF SELF IS *learned,* AND WE ARE *teaching* IT BY *being* IT.

This negative energy doesn't stay internalized—it comes out in every interaction you have. We express ourselves based on how we see ourselves. It's the law of expression. What you think about you defines the way you talk, the way you walk, how you stand, how you smile. The way you express or carry yourself affects the way other people perceive you. Energy speaks far louder than words. Some may not know exactly what it is they are sensing but may feel unable to trust you, sense your lack of confidence in what you are saying and perhaps challenge your viewpoint, or they may sense your doubt about yourself and keep their distance. One thing they know for sure is that you don't trust yourself. Imagine someone who walks into a room with the energy of confidence, self-assurance, a smile, and a comfort in themselves. You will be drawn to them—they're energy is electric! You can see how the opposite energy would cause the opposite reaction.

It took me a while to realize that it wasn't just about a few negative thoughts that would add up; it was the pattern in my thoughts. These patterns were learned. Every single time I believed what the media said about beauty and body size, I was programmed. Every time another kid made fun of me, the pattern cemented. Repetition shapes our beliefs. After all, it's easy to accept something as true if it's repeated often enough. All of all sudden, the negative things you hear become the negative things you say to yourself, and suddenly, they become your reality.

This was the case in 2019, when I hit a personal low. I felt deprived of life and love, as if the joy had been sucked out of me. I couldn't believe that even after losing over 100 lbs, I still wasn't good enough, successful enough, or pretty enough. This was combined with stressors such as my driver's license being taken away. I was physically unwell. In an effort to lose weight to meet what I thought beauty was, I was risking my health. When the weight came back, so did my feelings of failure. All the while, there were those familiar critics bouncing around in my head, telling me I was unworthy. I believed that more than ever.

In September of 2019, I finally tried something new. Instead of trying to change myself to be something I wasn't, I decided to question some of the beliefs I'd been expressing life through. What beliefs did I hold? Why had I been trying to lose weight my entire life. What would I gain? What would be the benefit? After some journaling and self-reflection, it came to me. I believed to be successful, to be loved, and to measure up, I needed to be in a thin body. Success was looking physically fit, working out at 5 am, wearing business suits, and looking perfect. At that moment, I realized that it did not need to be this way. I discarded every current (and false) idea of what it means to be successful. The abs, the business suits, the perfect smile—it all felt like a lie. It didn't feel authentic. Instead, I decided to be me. Maybe being "me" was the real path to success. I ended up proving this to be true. All these ideas about myself that I viewed as flaws were not the problem. The problem was believing they were flaws in the first place. I had been believing a story that was never my own.

After this epiphany, I realized I needed to stop trying to change my outside and start from the inside. This started me on my journey to real, genuine, and unconditional self-love. It all came down to this: Change your image of yourself, and you will create different and more fulfilling life experiences. I was willing to give it a try. What did I have to lose?

I started this journey by asking, what is love? How do we explain it? We likely all know what it feels like to love someone. We have experienced the warmth and comfort it provides. But often, love can be something that eludes us, something we feel is just outside our grasp, or something we long for more of. It has a mysterious power over us, and I don't think I ever really knew what love was.

This is especially true when trying to love yourself. It's hard to pin down exactly what this looks like in action. How should you talk to yourself? How should you change your perception? How do you find a healthy balance between positive self-talk and constructive criticism? This takes patience and proper guidance.

Much like I have my own definition of "best," I also see the path to self-love a little differently. While many see the move toward self-love as a mental shift and regard it as a highly intellectual process, I believe that true self-love involves more than just the mental plane. To feel fully requires a shift not only in the mind, but also in the body and spirit. When these align, you can start to put self-love into practice. Loving all parts of you, including your oneness to spirit, is key to creating real meaning and purpose to your life.

Learning proper self-love comes down to continual evolution and awareness. It means loving yourself regardless of the circumstances. It means loving yourself unconditionally. Instead of focusing on a less than ideal situation, you become present and feel the love and positivity in the present moment, and you are willing to direct it inward. You ask yourself, how is this a reflection of how I feel about me, rather than asking, why is this happening to me.

This can be easy but will require focused attention upon yourself and your own self-realization. It involves becoming aware of patterns of thought and actions you've grown accustomed to and choosing to see yourself in a new way, thus creating new patterns. Many will not put in the time and effort necessary for meaningful change because they either are not aware of the level of fulfillment available to them, or they aren't willing to really look at themselves and answer some of the tough questions.

Many people also put up walls to make sure this rebuilding process doesn't happen. After all, you've likely grown used to your internal monologue, even when it's degrading or unhealthy. To you, it's comfortable, and any change to move away from this would introduce chaos into your life. In response—maybe out of fear or an unwillingness to change—the part of you that seeks growth remains blocked off. You reach an upper limit in the love you hold for yourself and in your willingness to allow more love in.

This resistance to growth sits in your subconscious mind and will stay there until you replace it. Oftentimes, it stems from a genuine dislike of yourself. This was the case for me. I always believed I was flawed. For reasons you may not be fully aware of, you can't fathom owning yourself and finding confidence in your body. This was learned, whether it was an emotional impact that happened in your past or the constant internalization of what other people told you. As a result, you don't bother to show yourself love—it feels impossible or not worth pursuing.

On the other hand, some people believe the shift toward self-love is simple. As a result, their idea of self-love is often more shallow or superficial, as if you only need to tweak a few things or change your tone of voice and suddenly you love yourself. This is one of the biggest misconceptions about self-love. I compare this to the same person driving a different car. Sure, the situation has shifted and it might be shinier on the outside, but this change isn't substantial or sustainable. The vehicle makes a difference, but it doesn't last long unless you change the mindset of the driver. This happened to me over and over again. I would go on a diet, lose some weight, make some people proud in my life, and notice a flicker of self-love and a bout of confidence show up. But then, time would pass, weight would come back on or I would hit a plateau, and the thoughts of negativity would come right back. I would end up in front of the mirror being critical yet again.

This is common in the beauty and plastic surgery industry. You change your appearance but still never feel fully loved by yourself or by others. The quest to continue to change your appearance is ongoing, because the patterns of how you see yourself have remained the same.

Instead, it is important to dig deeper to find the root of the issue and to find the real value in who you really are. This process can be simple, and it can be joyful, but it will require discipline. You've spent years thinking you are flawed, that you are imperfect or damaged in a permanent way. This belief led you to manufacture a false image built off a concept or identity you see of yourself. Based on this viewpoint, you live your life as if you are faulty instead of special. This leaves you living in limbo, stuck in a gap between hating yourself and wanting to be different. It's up to you to leave this limbo. It's time to make a new decision.

It can be hard to leave behind the life you've built, the comfort of always knowing what to expect next, even if it's knowing things will stay the same. It's predictable and safe. You are potentially abandoning a version of yourself you have been with for a long time, and it's normal to question if you are ready to take the leap into the best of yourself. I can assure you, through my years of personal growth and development and in the years of mentoring others through theirs, it's absolutely worth it. YOU are worth it.

This "worth" became crystal clear during the pandemic and subsequent quarantine. With new mandates restricting how I lived, I had a shocking revelation: in some ways, I was already living my life like I was in quarantine. Sure, I was able to move more and not wear a mask before the pandemic, but I didn't really feel free to live the life I wanted. I was closed off and imposing restrictions on myself that, in retrospect, felt arbitrary. I would not dare consider becoming an entrepreneur because I never saw the possibility for me, just for others. I would think, "I'd love to work from home," yet I continued to work at a job that kept me out of the house for 12 hours a day.

I put up walls and set limits because I didn't want to consider my potential for change. I was unwilling to look outside of what I knew. Unsurprisingly, this unknowing box I had built kept me in the same place. Still, I was willing to settle in and make myself comfortable, separated from the chaos of the outside world. I would see other people going after their dream boldly and bravely, and I'd think "good for them." I'd even send them my encouragement, saying, "You can do it!" but I'd never speak that same way to myself.

This happens to a countless number of people. After years of regression, they put up barriers that block off their potential. They board up the windows and refuse to let light in. In some ways, this feels safer. They now have a schedule they can stick to with few surprises. The natural emotional highs and lows of life are dulled. They exist on a consistent plateau. They grow cozy with these constraints and are never challenged to seek more.

This *Matrix*-type of life would make anyone feel unfilled, yet they still can't pinpoint why they feel empty. They forget or are completely unaware that this cycle can be escaped. Once they do consider abandoning their routine and leading a new life, they repeat the same familiar excuses: *Change is too chaotic. I don't have enough time. I have too many responsibilities. I'm tired.* So the choice becomes to stay the same, and this complacency leads us toward disintegration instead of growth.

For some, this lack of self-love turns into depression. As soon as we start to identify as someone who is "depressed" or "has depression," we have essentially chosen an existence that keeps us down and limits our ability to really thrive. We start to run from ourselves, and we surrender to a less rewarding life. We get stuck in a feedback loop of negative self-talk instead of treating ourselves with the care we deserve. We stop wanting to be successful, and we settle for moments of happiness instead because we assume they will be fleeting.

After diving deep and allowing myself some self-reflection, I realized that, in a sense, I had chosen depression for many years. As a mother of two little girls, I was at home living a life in contrast to what I had hoped to achieve in my life. The cycle of doing the same routine every single day started to get to me. This caused a disconnect that disrupted every aspect of my being. I felt numb to the beauty around me. I was ungrateful for the life I'd built because I had allowed my mind to cycle through all the reasons I wasn't good enough, why my life wasn't good enough, and how the world wasn't what I hoped it would or could be. I set myself on a cycle of negativity and all I could see was the bad. The clouds skewed my vision. I was caught in the storm of my own negative thoughts, and I stopped being able to even see the possibility of the sun coming through the clouds.

This feeling remained until a pivotal moment in my journey toward self-love. In early 2020, I was ready to launch my coaching business. I wrote out a few notes about what kind of coach I wanted to be and the identity I desired to hold of myself. I wrote down, "150 lbs and workout at 5 am every day." I had been working on myself for a few months already, so my confidence was growing, and I was at a place where I was starting to question many beliefs I held. After I wrote this down, I asked myself, "Why do I believe I need to be at this weight or have this habit to be successful?"

After some introspection, I realized there was a certain image to aim for if you were a woman working as a coach. Most of the "successful coaches," both male and female, were slim, posted about early morning workouts, wore business suits (or suit dresses), were professionally put together with professional headshots, always smiling, etc. There was this very clear image in my mind of an executive-level appearance and approach. This appearance would make all the difference, because you would be taken seriously if you "appeared" to be successful yourself. After all, if you aren't impeccably put together, how can you give out advice? So for me, if you didn't look healthy, no one would hire you. At the time, nobody really discussed how unhealthy and restrictive this belief was. The old me would have entered another cycle of self-deprivation to appear like I measured up, all because I didn't see my worth in who I was.

After the realization of why I chose that statement, I decided to believe something else. I scratched it out and wrote, "I am beautiful and worthy of success in the body I am in NOW." This changed everything.

I decided for the first time in my life not to try to lose any weight, not to force myself to work out at 5 am if I didn't want to, and to just be ME. I decided to be authentically me. I decided not to wear business suits and blazers but to wear what felt like me. I decided to love my body and confidently speak in front of people with the confidence that I was worthy of taking up space. I decided to show my uniqueness, including my visible tattoos. I didn't mean to be subversive or disruptive, I just no longer tried to meet a societal standard. I decided to love myself to become the best of myself.

Of course, I was nervous. Leaving the comfort of believing I was forever flawed was uncomfortable at first, but I knew this was likely the one belief that if I changed, it would change my life, and it did. Very quickly, my confidence grew and the laws of attraction set in. People were refreshed with my authenticity and my realness, and they could see themselves in me. While others in the industry were slowly growing, I was leaping forward. Hundreds of people wanted to learn from me. Deciding to love myself as I was started a movement of others having permission to do the same.

I remember one woman approaching me after a session I did for other coaches. She pulled me aside, and with a tone of relief and respect, she simply said, "You proved me wrong." She had truly thought that someone like me couldn't triumph as a coach because of my body size. I had gone against the rigid standard for women and found success, showing other women in the industry what was possible. I didn't set out to do this. I used to try to fit into the mold myself. But it was going against the grain that helped me. I didn't need to actually change myself into a new person. I just needed to become who I authentically was and to live that new narrative.

Essentially, I took control back and built my own path to success. I started to listen to myself and found confidence in what I wanted. This was a huge step in escaping my *Matrix* type of life.

I remember my old way of self-improvement; it was led more by hate than by love. I refer to this as the "old way." Embarking on this journey, I have learned so much about myself and so much about personal growth and development. What I have come to believe is that love is always the answer. So, why do I think old models of personal growth and development are no longer working? Because they are built upon the same societal norms/values/ideals that limit us. We teach people how to be better by painting a picture of what perfect is, and when you don't meet that picture, you are broken, a problem needing fixing, or perpetually flawed. So, your quest for growth doesn't come from love but from a desire for the solution to your flaw. This old way has you call out your limit and your problem and make steps to change it. If you procrastinate, take action. If you are overweight, hire a trainer and go on a diet. If you don't have enough money, start a side business to make more. This cycle uses motivation and will power to create a new habit and instill a new behavior. Once we start to see results (deadlines met, weight loss, increased income), we start to feel good about ourselves, finally "measuring up." This is where we finally feel it's okay to love ourselves, to be confident, to give ourselves a pat on the back, because we fixed our problem...or did we? What ends up happening is we simply find another problem, or we go right back to our old behavior because we actually never fixed anything. In the end, we still believe we are broken. This cycle of growth is dependent upon results, and we only love ourselves when we give ourselves a command and follow, when we set goals and achieve them, and when we make other people proud. This is conditional, and I've known this cycle all too well.

The example I gave above about loving myself to find the best of myself started with self awareness. I started to look into what I actually believed about me, and whether I wanted to continue believing it. Whose beliefs were they? What if I no longer believed them to be true? This self-awareness was the starting point of a new growth cycle, an unconditional self-love cycle. After self-awareness, I chose self-love NOW. I turned my focus not on changing myself but on understanding who I really was and loving her. This is an important part of the growth cycle because you aren't focused on the problem or the gain; you are focused on your strengths. There is no better way to become better than by seeing how good you already are. You cannot experience more love unless you are more love. With this self-love underway, you will find a natural tendency to want to continue to grow and expand from a place of love. You will want to do more self-care, dress differently, spend more time on yourself, and become more aware. The shifting of habits will happen naturally to align with the best of yourself. You won't walk every day because you should but because you want to. You will choose health for the longevity of your vessel and not for your appearance. You will show up in your business/career more engaged because you want to be there and express yourself. The outcome of this growth is more self-love!

This improvement cycle isn't results-based; it's unconditional. You love yourself no matter what, whether your body meets an ideal, whether business success comes, whether you find your soul mate or not, etc. It's true detachment from any outcome, and it's true freedom. You still want to be the best of yourself, but you don't need to be. You learn your worth comes from within.

When I taught this growth cycle to my students this week, the question came up, "So how do I love myself more?" How do we move out of the comfort of self-criticism and move into self love?

I believe following these four steps will help you move into this place. Step 1: Understanding. Step 2: A new decision. Step 3: Introspection. Step 4: Cheerlead yourself.

The first step (understanding) is to become aware that so much of this exists in the mind and you have all the control. Ultimately, people become prisoners of their own mind. They are restrained by their thoughts and how they perceive themselves, and this creates the rules they live by. They build a box to keep out other possibilities and treat it like it's their shelter. One of my favorite quotes is from Neville Goddard: "The dramas of life are a psychological one." This is exactly what he is talking about. We perceive situations, people, and the world from the lens of our own identity (including our limitations), so we experience this life, good or bad, from who we believe we ARE.

Many believe that their thoughts come from their mind, that they have no control, and this stance makes you powerless. Accepting the belief that I control my thoughts was essential for my own growth. What I can control I can change. So what if you are controlling it all? Do you feel your power coming back?

The second step is to make a new decision. Familiarity makes us content. Even when we want something better, we fall back on familiarity. However, one of the first steps toward true self-love is to move beyond being content and to move into the desire to truly thrive. Life is not just to be lived but to be fully experienced. There are higher levels of everything for you to experience, but you are simply unaware of them. There is a higher level of love, of happiness, of joy, of peace, of fulfillment than even I have been able to experience yet, but I am committed to allowing myself to experience this entire fullness that life has to offer. So what if we don't want to just get through this life, but we want to love this life? It all starts with this decision to choose to love you first. This is a pivotal step in becoming the best of yourself. You are essentially choosing you.

WE
experience
THIS LIFE,
good OR *bad*,
FROM WHO WE
believe
WE ARE

The next step is introspection. Through your self-awareness, you can notice the clutter and clear it out. Having a clear head leads to more fulfilling self-love.

Start by asking yourself some questions:

Who am I, truly?
What pisses me off?
What am I afraid of?
What am I ashamed of?
What am I proud of?
What are my strengths?
What would make me better?

With each answer, feel free to dive in as deep as you're comfortable. As you answer, strip away your influences. Get to the root of you outside of the context of community, of the "other," which I will speak about in the next chapter. The irony here is that you have to go deep within to get out. Stop looking outside yourself and start the journey within yourself.

This often starts with discarding the pain from your past. Otherwise, it is easy to ruminate and get stuck in the same thought cycles. Sure, it's important to remember that your past experiences led to where you are today, but they don't define you. You also can't create a new identity based entirely on your past or your memories. You can consider this as part of your person, but if it doesn't affect you now, there's no need to conjure it up. Instead, you can access your higher intellectual faculties. So I would ask the question, is this really who I am or simply who I THINK I am. The best of yourself is about discarding other people's beliefs about you and replacing them with your own.

The final step to more self-love is to give yourself the attention you have always deserved. Stand in front of that mirror and tell yourself what you would tell your best friend. Become your own cheerleader. When you notice an unkind thought toward yourself, talk back to yourself like your mother would if she heard you say that to yourself. Take ownership of every thought, and discipline yourself to lift yourself up. Give yourself grace and empower yourself to see the greatness that is within. A simple "I love you, Kathleen" has made all the difference for me. I'm certain it will for you too.

As you discover some newfound confidence, it takes a careful balance and a lot of checking in to see where your head is at and if your thinking patterns are healthy. Some of this confidence can feel foreign to you and uncomfortable. Stay the course. Think about kids and changing their bedtime for back-to-school preparation. They put up a fight, but you hang tight and eventually they fall into the new time or new pattern. You will fall into the new pattern. You might fight yourself, but let the best of you win.

How do we make sure your self-love isn't narcissistic or egotistical? Can you love yourself too much? Many people think they love themselves when they are really embodying—and emboldening—their ego. They might show to the world that they love themselves but really they only hope to. This over-inflated sense of confidence actually stems from a lack of confidence. They want to show you they are confident, but deep down inside, they are their own worst critic. Sometimes the ego tries to fool you too. The "human" part of you and your mind tells you that because you have a lot of followers, because you made a lot of money, because you have nice cars that you are good, successful, and measure up. But real self-love is being proud of yourself without all that fluff. Self-love goes hand in hand with acceptance, grace, and forgiveness.

Real self-love involves connecting with your spirit, your oneness, your divinity. By seeing what you really are, you don't get fooled by a false image of self-love that is supported by society. Let's drop the need to fit in, to measure up, and to prove ourselves, and let's move into the act of finding our real selves and being at peace.

When practicing self-love, it's important to know what it isn't. It's not measuring yourself against others and wondering how worthy you are in comparison. It isn't about getting what you need from other people. It's about saying yes to yourself and feeling it. It isn't about competing; it's about collaborating. It isn't about being a productive member of society, but it's about answering the call within you, from the divine. The feeling lingering within you—that you were made for more—that's the real you. Your infinite potential is calling you. Are you willing to listen?

THE *feeling* LINGERING WITHIN YOU— THAT YOU *were* MADE FOR *more* —THAT'S THE *real* YOU.

CHAPTER 2:
Journal Prompts

Reflect on your relationship with self-love: How do you currently navigate the ups and downs of life while maintaining a sense of love and acceptance for yourself? Are there specific circumstances or challenges that test your ability to practice self-love? How can you expand your awareness and enhance your understanding of self-acceptance in those moments?

Uncover the barriers to self-love: Are any recurring patterns or thought patterns hindering your ability to embrace and love yourself in all circumstances fully? Identify any underlying beliefs or fears that contribute to these barriers. How can you challenge and overcome these obstacles to foster a deeper sense of self-love and acceptance?

Evolve your self-love practice: Reflect on the strategies and tools you currently utilize to cultivate self-love during triumphs and hardships. Can you explore new approaches or practices to deepen your self-acceptance journey? Consider incorporating self-compassion exercises, gratitude practices, or mindfulness techniques to further develop your understanding and experience of self-love in various situations.

CHAPTER **THREE:**

The "Other"

As I formulated ideas for this book, I considered the best approach to personal growth and development that I could share with my readers. I thought about what "self-help" really means. It suddenly struck me that it wasn't just about *self*-improvement—our best also involves improving the lives of others any way that we can. After all, how can we talk about bettering ourselves without considering other people?

We often become the best version of ourselves by helping others become the best version of themselves. This growth happens in tandem. After our service to others, they in turn give back and shape our journey. As we progress and change and grow, the presence of other people lingers in our mind. We wonder how other people influence us, how they don't influence us, how they guide our thoughts and actions. This can be enlightening as well as damaging. Either way, the weight of other's words and actions will be there.

We don't live in isolation; there are always going to be other people. With this in mind, we have to consider the "other" on the journey to our best. More specifically, we need to consider how we engage with and understand the "other" and how they can help or hurt our sense of self.

Who or what is the "other"?

It is anyone or anything other than yourself. While this "other" exists outside of your mind, body, and spirit, it still influences how you live. Your mind is always exposed to other's experiences and opinions. This external world shapes how you see yourself and the way you act; oftentimes, it can become more powerful than your internal monologue.

In countless ways, your life is defined by the other. We are always questioning how we will be perceived or how we measure up when compared to our community. Before making any decision, we wonder how others will react. What will other people think? What are other people doing? How does it differ from what I'm doing? These questions can consume us if we let them. They can make us go against our gut feeling or second guess every decision.

You exist around others, exposed for their inspection. You aren't just one person alone on this planet. Unless you live a life of complete solitude, the other is impossible to escape. Humans, after all, are social creatures. We crave attention and interaction. The individual mind needs stimulation—it cannot exist without culture and relationships. You can seclude yourself as long as you'd like, but you'd eventually grow lonely and unfulfilled. To truly be human means you are active in society, engaging with people, and willing to be judged by others; otherwise, how would you measure success?

When observed by the other, we have the choice to change our actions to appear successful. We might put on a performance to make ourselves look "better" than we actually are. We might laugh a little louder, stand a little taller, smile a little bigger, and stretch the truth a bit, all while thinking this will show us at our best. While this behavior is understandable, it is inauthentic. You are trying to show yourself at your best instead of simply being yourself at your best.

More often than not, people will see through the act.

Still, as we aspire to be our best selves, we can't help but be on display. Most changes you make to better yourself become public. Others see the different versions of you—how you've changed over the years or from day to day. Likewise, you see different versions of them. All the while, there's an unavoidable judgment as you size each other up and see where you stand in the social hierarchy.

This judgment can be damaging. It can make us feel inferior in the eyes of others. We might feel at peace when we're alone, but once another person enters our space, everything shifts. Sometimes, it feels like the air is sucked out of the room. Depending on the person and the circumstance, you change the way you behave. You measure if they are a friend or a threat and act accordingly. You might be loud and goofy when you're comfortable, or shy and serious when threatened. This all shapes how you are perceived.

While identity remains in the mind, a large part of your identity is shaped by these interactions with the "other." It isn't made in isolation. This influence from the other is mutual—the way you act around others shapes them as well. You have the power to shape other people just like they have the power to change how you act.

Part of this influence comes from how you compare yourself to them. You might wonder how you shape up when next to this other person and what you should do to make yourself similar. This could stem from feelings of envy or jealousy. You want what they have so you think you need to be like them, so you change your behavior. The more you are pushed to be someone else, the less authentic you become.

French philosopher Jean-Paul Sartre once stated, "The Other is simultaneously the one who has stolen my being from me and the one who causes 'there to be' a being which is my being." (Solomon 245) In other words, the influence of other people can make you inauthentic, but without them, you wouldn't really exist. Social interactions shape who you are, but they move you away from your true self.

This creates conflict. How can you be your best authentic self while still being a part of a community? How can you ignore the urge to compare yourselves to others and instead be fully attuned with yourself?

Instead of being a source of envy, the "other" can forge a path to success. Think about it this way: when you compare yourself with others, you are building a narrative. There is a story you write in the space between you and this other person. It is a story that centers on your differences, how your paths diverge, how your personality differs, and what it would take for you to become this other person or to achieve the same kind of success.

As you write this story, you have an option: either you make the narrative detrimental or you make it beneficial.

You can choose to compare yourself to the other in a healthy way and make your story optimistic. It all depends on your mindset and how you frame the situation.

I'm sure you've been told that only bad things can come from comparing yourself to others and that it's a practice you should stop, or that you should stop caring about what other people are doing with their lives.

This is easier said than done. After all, isn't it a normal, healthy function to judge yourself in relation to others? In some instances, isn't it inspiring?

The goal here isn't to stop comparing yourself to others completely. Not only is this aim impossible to attain, but it might actually be detrimental.

Instead of a detractor, I see comparison as a useful tool. Comparing yourself to the "other" can be a way to discover yourself. You see who you are in relation to other people and the influence that they have on you. Once you have some perspective, you can take and apply the parts that you like and leave the parts that you don't.

We can either compare ourselves to others to make us feel empowered, or we can do it to make us feel as though we are less than. When we measure ourselves against the achievements of others, we naturally remind ourselves of the negative. This is especially true if we want to become like them, or achieve what they have achieved. If we aspire to be more like someone else, we imagine all the obstacles: *This is going to be hard. This is going to be such a challenge. I don't think it's worth doing.* When we assume this, we make this negativity happen. Our failure is a self-fulfilling prophecy.

Let's say you compare yourself to someone else who is in your same industry and you think they may be doing better than you. Maybe they are making more money, or they're more well known within the same sphere. When we do this we suddenly have feelings that might feel like your self-worth plummeting. You now feel "less than." You feel insecure. You might even feel a little sick to your stomach. There's a physical and emotional response that affects your mood and makes you less motivated. You stop what you are doing and think, "why even bother trying."

On the other hand, if you compare yourself to the thousands of other people in your industry out there who <u>aren't</u> touching what you're doing, then you feel good. You begin to feel secure with yourself and know you're on the right path. You are then willing to keep moving forward, and maybe even feel an inspired action moment take hold. You can do this with every aspect of your life, whether it's your career, your finances, or your social circle. Put your achievements into perspective relative to others and focus on the positive.

Ultimately, when you compare yourself to others, it should be coming from a place of gratitude, of accomplishment, of gain, instead of dwelling on what you lack. It should be a way to boost your spirit and your ego, not deflate it.

Part of this comes down to changing the language you use. Don't think of it as a comparison; instead, you are using someone else as a <u>frame of reference</u>. This way, you are not in competition with the other person. Competition breeds comparison, but respect creates a frame of reference. You are relating yourself to the other, using the law of relativity in your favor. Nothing is good or bad, but our judgment makes it so. When we compare something to the thing next to it, we decide if it's good or bad, high or low, big or small. So, let's compare ourselves in an empowering way, and use this law for good.

Before we dive into these ideas further, I want to share my own relationship with comparing myself to others and how it helped and hurt my success.

When I joined Bob Proctor's world as a consultant, I decided to launch my business partnering with him and using his program within my coaching package. The investment to do so was the biggest I'd ever made in myself before, costing over $40,000. I saw this as a sound investment, especially because I was just starting out. I figured if I could use Bob's well-known credibility and his course, I would be successful.

Over the coming months, I started to study myself more. After some introspection, I asked myself: Who do I want to be as a coach? What are my strengths? What are my weaknesses? How do I want to teach this material?

These questions made me more focused and intentional. I ended up becoming more and more unique and individual, doing things in ways no one else was doing them. I took my approach to affiliate marketing and attraction marketing and applied it in my business. I was growing fast and doing it all online, something not many were doing. I ended up selling Bob's program so fast that I was breaking records within his organization. I didn't even realize just how abnormal this level of fast success really was. To my surprise, this created a buzz with other consultants and coaches in the industry, and my inbox started filling up with questions, meeting requests, and celebratory messages. The organization celebrated me, and I am aware now just how much this "star" feeling boosted me up.

In under one year, I received my Diamond Pin. I was the fastest one to receive it in the history of Bob's company. I was elated. I would tell you that I couldn't believe the progress I'd made in such a short amount of time, but that would be untrue; I expected it. I applied what Bob and additional mentors taught me, and I convinced myself it was already done.

A beautiful awareness came for me on a celebratory Zoom call in January 2021. I got all dressed up and ready to receive my Diamond Pin on the Inner

Circle call. I had just qualified for my Diamond Pin the week before on January 4, so I was really excited and proud to be on and to speak about how I had done it in such a short time. I was so excited to inspire others through my growth. But something happened that I did not expect. As the event started, the director of the program started out by saying, "This celebration is for those who qualified up until December 31 of 2020, so Kathleen, we will celebrate you next quarter." This would mean that I would be celebrated in three months. This accomplishment that I literally gave my life to was being pushed off for three months. While I could feel my emotions bubbling up, I had to compose myself. I couldn't show my sadness on a Zoom full of people. Before the Zoom was even over, my phone started blowing up with texts from people in the Zoom who couldn't believe what they were hearing.

After I left the Zoom, I sat back, took a deep breath, and considered what had just unfolded. I was surprised at how upset I was. It really hurt me. I asked myself: "Why is this bothering me so much?" After some journaling, I had the awareness that outside recognition is something I need to feel successful, to feel whole, to feel loved. It wasn't enough to give myself the pat on the back, I still needed it from others. I desperately desired the validation of the "other." Without it, my achievement didn't feel real. I felt I wasn't worthy without that feedback. For the first time in a while, I felt small. What did I do this for?

In that moment, I was being the "best" of myself to make other people proud. It wasn't an internal drive to be better or to do more for me. Still, I remained under the influence of the "other" and let this dictate my feelings. I replaced wanting to make my father proud with the desire to make Bob proud. Through this situation I realized that I am all the validation I really need, that following my own lead, giving myself praise and loving who I am in this moment was more than enough and I let it go. No one wronged me, nothing was unfair, it all happened for my growth, truly.

This awareness was big for me. Once I shifted this, I started to do things for me in a way that made me feel good. I started teaching this material in my own way, creating my own intellectual property, launching some of my own courses, and even starting my own methodologies. These models were helping people thrive in huge ways, and the world was resonating, because I was really stepping into who I really was, not comparing myself.

Finally, in September of 2021, I launched my own course completely separate from Bob. It was called "Millionaire," and it captured my own approach to coaching. It was spirituality meets personal growth and development, and it was the roadmap I took to create millions of dollars in just one year. By now, I believed enough in my intellectual property, my growth, and the results I'd seen to forge ahead solo. I ended up selling twice as many programs than I'd ever sold in a month selling Bob's program. Becoming the best of myself propelled me forward. I was me, and it was more than enough.

My journey with Bob's company ended abruptly in January 2022, right before Bob's passing. While it was uncomfortable, I knew at that moment that I had grown enough to really step into who I was and to "go it alone." I was freed to truly be the real me in that moment, and it felt great. I am grateful for that call and the path it led me down. Everything really does happen for our greater good.

Another beautiful example of how to positively use the presence of "others" is when I choose to observe others as a source of <u>inspiration</u> instead of competition.

When I first launched my coaching business, I had done some work on myself and noticed that when I would see others achieve big things, it made me feel a bit low. Comparing myself to them didn't feel good and made me feel behind. So one thing I intentionally did was to look at others' successes as inspiration. There were two women who were Bob Proctor consultants who had built multi-million dollar businesses. I intentionally told myself, "If they can do it, then so can I." This was the first time I actually believed it. I wasn't less than; I was equipped with the same spirit, mind, and body. I saw what they did and felt inspired to do the same. I focused on what they were doing and began using them as a frame of reference. They were the example that pushed me toward my own success. They were the "other" that enabled me to build a more successful identity and eventually become what I was seeing outside of me.

As my journey progressed, I only paid attention to those doing more than me in an inspired state. I later discovered that only a small percentage of Bob Proctor consultants around the world achieved this level of success. Can you imagine if I had used that as a frame of reference? I would have unknowingly selected the manifestation of slow and resistive success instead of the magic that unfolded from me. So to this day, when I see someone else achieving more than me, I immediately think, "Yes! That's more evidence for me."

It's as simple as this: if we assume others will fail in something that we want, we put ourselves in the same situation. Unsurprisingly, we're more likely to reach the same outcome. If we instead align ourselves with success, we have a path toward it ourselves. This all stems from framing our comparisons to others in a positive way.

Through healthy framing, I was able to become inspired, not envious. I was motivated instead of self-deprecating. I received recognition and was able to frame it positively instead of brushing it off. It's not bad to be recognized or to receive positive feedback, but notice how you are when you don't get it. Are you dependent upon it, versus it being a nice bonus to your life? For me, it was more about getting in other people's proximity instead of being envious of what they had and what I lacked.

When doing so, make sure you don't take that frame of reference too far. You don't want to give other people or situations too much power. It can become a crutch. To allow other people to be the reason for your success or your demise reiterates the "other" having control over your situation. It ignores your autonomy. After those people are gone, who will you rely on? How does your business keep growing? At the end of the day, it's only you.

The reality with which you reside in, is entirely up to you. Everything still comes back to you, even if you don't build your concept of "self" alone. Our individual consciousness still determines what we bring to our lives and how we enact our freedom. I have not built the life I have on my own, which means I didn't do it alone, but I control the one thing I know I can, which is me.

After all is said and done, I believe my success is caused by me and emits from me. Even if I say I let someone else influence me, it was still my decision to be influenced. Every imagined scenario, every thought, every action (or lack thereof) was my choice.

Apart from not giving the "other" too much power, it helps to keep your frame of reference realistic. Do I see myself at the same level as Oprah? Not exactly. But this level of success is very attainable and reachable if you believe it is.

Still, what if I do want to be on the same level as Oprah some day? The first step is to <u>take your idols off the pedestal</u>. They are people. They aren't superheroes.

When you put someone up on a pedestal, you are saying that they have something that you can't possibly achieve. You end up treating them like they're an alien instead of someone you could aspire to be. To combat this, close the gap between how you see yourself and how you see this other person. Note your similarities and how close you are to reaching a similar version of success. Think about what aspect of them you <u>are</u> able to grasp. Once you do this, the idea of achieving Oprah-level success doesn't seem as farfetched. It just takes more steps to make it there. You can't climb Mt. Everest in one day; it takes patience. With this in mind, make the frame of reference you use manageable.

It might be better to start with someone in your orbit who inspires you. Consider a leader in your life. This could be a parent, a boss, a mentor, a teacher, or anyone occupying a position of influence whom people follow. They have the ability to guide others with their behavior. As the other, they influence you and you choose to become a follower. "Whatever you do, I'll follow suit."

This leader/follower relationship often stems from respect. You simply like how they live or how they lead, so you look up to them and take on aspects of their personality. As a follower, there's less comparison and more <u>inspiration</u>. The leader serves as a solid frame of reference. This is a lot healthier than being in competition.

In your life, you often have the choice to frame someone as a peer or as a leader. You wonder, is this person my competition? Or is this someone I simply look up to? Do I want to be better than this person, or do I want them to guide me? Both have their place, and both can be motivating. Still, having a frame of reference is better for your mental health.

I picture a hypothetical situation where a similar author launches their book on the same day as me. In this instance, I may immediately digress into comparison. This might consume my thoughts. *Whose book is going to be better? Who will sell more? Who's going to get more acclaim?* While this can be motivating in a way, it could fill me with negative energy. If I viewed this author instead as a peer or valued leader, I wouldn't feel this way. I would be more open to a simultaneous book launch. I'd see it as a positive experience. *How honored am I to launch my book at the same time!*

As you use others as a frame of reference, it's important to strike a careful balance. It's not healthy to be full of yourself when you think of yourself in relation to another person. It doesn't help to look down on others or see yourself as superior. In this case, you're inflating your ego in a way that prevents you from being your best. The pros and cons of the ego are something we'll explore in a later chapter. For now, simply find inspiration in other people instead of seeing them as less than. No one is better than you, but you also aren't better than anyone else. It goes both ways.

Making a frame of reference gives you actionable steps toward the best version of yourself that you can build off of <u>now</u>. It doesn't dictate every moment moving forward. It simply makes it easier to relate where you are currently with where you want to be in the future. After you practice comparing yourself to the "other" in a healthy way, you will learn how to naturally stop and start these comparisons as you see fit. In this way, you have control over the judgment of others and only use it to your advantage.

We are often told that you shouldn't care what people think, or that the opinions of others aren't helpful. There is some wisdom here. But again, is it really possible to stop considering other people's opinions? I would say it isn't feasible entirely, and we don't necessarily want to never care. It's about listening to the person who will give you the advice you're asking for, especially in business. This is where coaches and mentors are imperative in life. They give you advice based on either where they are or where you are going, instead of from where you are. And it's equally as important to listen to those who challenge you to grow in the direction you desire to go. When we hit an upper limit, we may subconsciously ask for advice from someone we know will tell us not to grow or who will feed into our fear. So choose wisely.

Still, you see it performed by people all the time. Someone aloof and indifferent openly states that they don't care what people think. However, the moment someone tells them, "You're doing an amazing job," they take this compliment and feel whole having received it. While it was a positive thought, they still cared what somebody thought about them. It's common sense—we like hearing nice things about ourselves. Some more than others. This is especially true if your love language is words of affirmation. This positive judgment makes you feel wanted and loved.

This good feeling is coming from the "other." It wouldn't exist unless someone else brought it into the world. Is that being the best of yourself if it doesn't come from within?

I don't think it's realistic to say, "From here on out, I don't need recognition ever again. I'm not going to care what people think from this point forward." You can't just quit cold turkey. Instead, you need to approach it with patience.

It's about climbing the levels of belief like a ladder until you reach the best of yourself. Imagine each step as a rung that you can't skip on your way up. With this mindset, your journey to the top becomes more manageable.

As you climb the ladder of belief, self-awareness is pivotal. You cannot change something about yourself you aren't even aware of. How many times do you see qualities in others that you know for a fact they would not see in themselves? They lack self-awareness. When you become more self-aware, you begin to question your ideals and obstacles regarding the input of others: *Where do I need recognition in my life? How much do I need the outside input? How important is it to me? Would I notice it if it were gone? Do I make my own decisions or allow others to make them for me?*

You can also question yourself in relation to others. *How often do I compare myself? How often do I care what people think when I put myself out in the world? How often do they negative opinions of others bother me? How do I deal with critique? How do I respond to positivity or compliments?*

This self-awareness is so important, and just as important to understand are the different levels of awareness. You can self-assess based on these, but ensure you are honest with yourself. There is no point in fooling yourself into a higher level. As you climb these levels of awareness, you can see your progression.

The following levels of awareness stem from the Barrett model, which itself was inspired by Maslow's hierarchy of needs (7 *Levels of Consciousness*; Gallagher).

1.Survival Instinct/Animal

This is existence at the primal level. You focus on food, health, and shelter. Little else occupies your mind. It is proto-social and has little to do with the "other" outside your community helping you survive.

2. Being in the Masses

You are a functioning, unquestioning member of society. You want to be like everyone else and you care what they think. You aspire to look the same, wear the same clothes, and do whatever you can do to avoid sticking out in the crowd. In a sense, it is other people that fill your cup, and you need them around to do so. You haven't yet discovered how to fill your own cup. I remember being in this level of awareness for much of my life; the desire to fit in was so strong. My young daughters are in this place—tweens all dressing the same and loving the same music and shows.

3. Aspiration

The seed planted that makes you yearn for more. Here, you may start to rebel and break away from the masses. You consider a separate path where you question the world and its arbitrary rules. This level is when you desire more and you start to really see that not being like everyone else might actually be how you will get it. This is where you start to connect with what YOU really want in life, instead of what you have been programmed to want.

4. Individual

This level of awareness is reached when you want to be yourself. You no longer desire to fit in. It is you at your most provocative because you are discovering a more authentic self, and you are willing to make changes to achieve it. What other people think is no longer as important, regardless of whether their opinions are positive or negative.

5. Discipline

This level of awareness is powerful because you start to see that the path to the realization of the best of yourself is through discipline. It's about choosing to be this version of yourself even when the world tries to convince you otherwise. We will always have these rhythms of life, but to remain thinking from the end, discipline in who you are being is key. This involves discipline in the ideas you think from, the thoughts you consistently have, the regulation of your emotional state, and the actions you choose to make. This disciplined version of you is unstoppable.

6. Experience

I have learned that I am someone who teaches from experience, not necessarily from concept. It's my own stories, experiences, and knowledge/wisdom that allow me to fully understand and apply what I teach and to become the embodied version of myself. In order to reach this level of awareness, it's imperative that you allow yourself to experience what it's like to be the best of yourself.

7. Mastery

This level of awareness happens when you "are" who you desire to be. This is "being", and is now your natural state. This happens with ease and flow. Old routines for reprogramming likely aren't needed, and the structures set in the mechanical system start to feel daunting. You act on intuition and internal desire rather than "shoulds." The other and the outside 3D world have less impact, and you find your triggers are completely gone. This is a place of peace.

As you work your way up these levels, you are rising above the influence of the other. You don't need the validation of your peers to feel good about yourself, but you can still use the other to your advantage as a frame of reference. Paying attention to where you sit here can create a seismic shift in the way you live. For example, moving away from the need for recognition and achieving mastery can change your love language. Words of affirmation, physical touch, and quality time are tied up in the other. Another person desires you enough to touch you or spend time with you. They like you enough to buy you a gift or say something nice about you. It is freeing to no longer need this outside influence to feel validated. When you love yourself enough, you don't need validation from others.

We aren't alone on this journey. There is always an outside influence, whether we like it or not. We have no choice but to understand how we work with others to best understand ourselves. We have to understand how the "other" influences who we are and how they can provide validation and a frame of reference.

While I want to inspire others and share my advice, I'm not going to teach you how to be more like me or to model me. I'm going to teach you to tap into the real you and to build the life you want. So many times I see people following in others' footsteps, but I want to encourage you to blaze your own damn trail and to do it with bravery and boldness in who you are.

WHEN YOU *love* *yourself* ENOUGH, YOU DON'T NEED *validation* FROM OTHERS.

CHAPTER 3:
Journal Prompts

Reflect on the power of uplifting others: Share a specific instance where you have witnessed or experienced the positive impact of helping someone else become their best self. How did this support or guidance contribute to your personal growth? How can you continue to embrace the idea of empowering others to enhance your journey toward self-improvement?

Explore the challenges and benefits of engaging with the "other": Identify a relationship or interaction in your life where you have experienced positive and negative effects on your sense of self. Reflect on the lessons learned from this experience and how they shaped your understanding of the "other." How can you navigate these dynamics in a way that allows for personal growth while maintaining healthy boundaries?

Redefine your concept of the "other": Challenge your current perception of the "other" by considering alternative perspectives. Are there groups, individuals, or ideas you have previously dismissed or misunderstood? How can you actively seek to understand and engage with these others in a way that promotes mutual growth and empathy? Reflect on the potential impact this expanded perspective can have on your journey toward becoming the best version of yourself.

CHAPTER **FOUR:**

Being, Not Becoming

In their efforts towards self-improvement, many people measure their concept of self from today against their best concept of themselves that exists somewhere in the future. From here, they believe they can become the better version of themselves. They think that who they were yesterday was not bad, but still, they can strive for better to reach the next level. This is a healthy way of starting this journey.

This is often tied up in the idea of the "future me"—that fuzzy image of you that exists at some unforeseeable time, in some unforeseeable place, achieved in some unforeseeable way. Oftentimes, people frame it like it's a fantasy: "In the future, I'll be confident. In the future, I'll be content with my career. In the future, I'll know my true purpose."

I am very cautious of the use of the word "future" when referring to the self. This word implies that it is something you currently are not and will later become. This focus on the "future me" also devalues who you are today.

Instead of looking to the future to feel good about yourself, give yourself self praise, appreciation, empowerment, and grace in the present. Ignore the idea of the "before and after" and the way that society pushes this idea. It ruins your potential for growth and the incredible power you have right now. Instead, envision your progress as perpetual growth, from good to great, from amazing to even better, from loving yourself to becoming the best of yourself. When we use the word *future*, we are keeping this version of us in the future. It is who you really are, and always have been, that is the best of yourself. The focus is on who you see yourself as NOW, not in the future.

This often comes clear in one's awareness when they embark on a goal-setting journey, as we look at creating a new life for ourselves. When we start asking for more, we go within and become aware of what limits us, what holds us back, and how we keep ourselves small. Realize that you are already in a good place. Everyone has experienced the harshness of our physical 3D world and has been molded by it, but we can heal. We can become aware of a stronger version of ourselves, a more resilient, more focused, more efficient, and more effective way of being. We can have all this and still move forward, and we can still love ourselves in the moment.

As we move through life, we often forget to zoom out and question how we see ourselves. I never considered the following questions before my personal growth and development journey started. Maybe you can ponder these quickly and see what immediately comes up for you.

Who am I?

How do I describe myself?

If someone wanted to know more about me, what would I tell them?

At its core, identity is the overall way in which you describe yourself or identify who you are.

IT IS WHO YOU *really* ARE, AND *always* *have* BEEN, THAT IS THE BEST OF *yourself*.

This can also be referred to as your self-concept. Becoming the best of yourself means living in your truth and enacting your authenticity. But how do you know what's true? How can you tell what's authentic? What are the building blocks that make up who you are?

To know your identity, you first need to evolve your understanding of your true self. This starts with introspection and considering the role of the intellectual mind.

First, reflect on everything that you bring into your life and what you are conscious of. Consider what you think and feel, how you behave, what you believe to be true. Reflect on your purpose and what pushes you and piques your interest. What drives you? What repels you? What do you take pride in? Conversely, what would you like to change?

Next, think about yourself in relation to the "other." Become conscious of how you are perceived and identified. Would others agree with your reflection and assessment of yourself? Does your idea of your authentic self line up with their idea of you? How much of yourself actually stems from them?

As you answer these questions, you might say you're considering your self-image. This is often the language used in the self-help world. I was first taught the concept of self image early on, and it resonated with me. It was something I could picture—there's an image I hold about myself that I can visualize in my mind's eye. The image I hold of myself then influences how I'm behaving every single day. In a sense, this image is my attempt at a visual representation of my success mechanism, showing me where that mechanism is set to, and thus showing me the path forward.

The more I sat with the word self-image, the more I felt it didn't fit. Is your perspective of self just an image? Isn't that oversimplifying it? How does this capture the complexity of the self? I now find this language to be restrictive. I believe your understanding of self exists beyond the image. It fails to account for self-concept and doesn't consider the internal data stored in the mind. I use language that I find is easily understood and feels light. When I think of self-image, I immediately go to body image or to visual representations

76

of my appearance, but the expansion past what we physically look like is critical. You are not your body, and thus focusing on this only limits your true potentiality.

More than just the image, your conception of self involves the "idea." After all, when it comes down to it, the way you see yourself is an idea. It's a narrative that you're writing in real time. What this means is the way in which you identify yourself and the concept you hold of yourself determines what your life is going to be like. You think from your assumptions. Whatever you determine to be true about yourself will then become the truth. With this in mind, you express yourself based on the beliefs that you hold.

For example, one aspect of your identity may be that you procrastinate. You may even go so far as to label yourself a procrastinator. This labeling links this practice with your identity. Your body literally follows through on what your mind tells it, and you're telling it to put things off and to NOT take action. With this idea in place, you will either continue to procrastinate or attempt to not procrastinate, while ending up eventually procrastinating again. We always go back to what we believe to be true about ourselves. Either way, <u>you are identifying yourself as a procrastinator</u>, and may say you are "trying not to." While you are trying not to, you are still identifying as someone who procrastinates so nothing changes. The easy thing to do is to continue to procrastinate. You have trained yourself to have that on automatic.

In order to rid yourself of procrastination in an effortless and natural way, you can easily replace the self-concept of procrastination with the identity of someone who takes action. This belief has to change at the fundamental (subconscious) level in order for your body to automatically act out a new belief about itself. In this way, you're not forcing yourself to change your behavior. Instead, you shift your entire self-concept, and your body follows. It then becomes natural for you to take action. Before you know it, you have let the procrastinator go, and you will wonder how you ever believed that about yourself before. Changed habits are temporary, but a changed identity is permanent (until you decide to become aware of an even more elevated version of you).

Identity is critical. As long as you believe you are a beginner at something, you will vibrate and behave that way. As long as you believe you are a coach trying to find clients, you will stay in that place. If you see yourself as unhealthy and trying to be healthy, you will stay there. It's the moment you believe you ARE an expert, you ARE a successful coach, you ARE healthy that it all shifts. What you are conscious of being today is what you will be observe tomorrow. So many stay in the becoming and never just BE.

Where does this change of self-concept start? It all begins with the understanding of the energy we emit.

There is a vibration that resonates with the concept you hold of yourself. You could say this is the emotional conception of self. It sends out energy based on your mood in the moment and it is a constant transmission of your identity. In a sense, your self-perception has a vibrational equivalent. This means that you <u>attract </u>or <u>repel </u>energy from your sense of self. You behave from it. You think from it. You feel from it. This action will continue indefinitely and forever become your reality. It dictates the world you live in.

When you change your concept of identity, you change the vibrational state that you're in. If the vibration is in alignment, it produces an equivalent vibration that causes attraction. From here, you shape your reality and progress toward what you deem ideal.

Of course, this can attract both positive and negative outcomes. You might have heard about some people who win the lottery and spend all the money they won and end up right back where they started. This is because they never changed the concept they held of themselves. Their identity remained the same, and they never adopted a new identity to match the new reality, so they ended up back in a life that resembled the one they had before they won the lottery. They never vibrationally changed who they were.

Whether the outcome is good or bad, you always have an identity. You are always thinking and acting from an idea of yourself. It's inescapable. You can't not have an opinion about yourself.

Naturally, if you believe that you aren't worthy, then you think from that place, you feel from that place, you vibrate from that place. Overall, you interact with the world as if you were unworthy. This translates as negative self-talk: "I don't think I'll get that job so I won't bother applying." "I don't know enough to start that business." "I'm not confident enough to perform live in front of an audience." Some people don't even notice how unworthy they truly believe they are until they start to love themselves more. Once you start to see what self-love is, you become more aware of the self-judgments. It's not who you are that manifests; it's who you THINK you are or what you THINK about who you see yourself as.

To combat this, a journey of self-discovery will be required in order to first find out who you are and to realize what parts of you could be empowered. Self-awareness is always the beginning of this journey.

This is difficult when there are so many distractions and outside influences. We are constantly getting suggestions from those around us—our family, the media, our peers. How we see ourselves is simply a culmination of other people's thoughts and ideas. Someone called me sensitive, and I accepted it. Someone called me fat and lazy, and I believed it. Someone told me I was a C student, and I took it hook, line, and sinker.

This idea of "report card syndrome" was an interesting idea when I first heard about it, and it helped me to understand this concept better. What we get on our report card is often how we will continue to show up in the world. So for kids, it's a literal report card, but for times later in life, it's your performance review at your job, it's your friend's opinions of who they think you are, it's your parents' work ideals engrained in how you show up at work.

IT'S NOT WHO
YOU ARE THAT
manifests;
IT'S WHO YOU
THINK YOU ARE

This was an idea I resonated with deeply. When I was in school, I started getting Bs and Cs. Regardless of the class, it was a struggle to achieve an A. Over time, the Bs and Cs increased, and I eventually accepted this as my truth. These grades defined my identity, I didn't think I was smart or exceptional. I had resigned to being moderate in all I did, so I applied myself moderately. Unsurprisingly, I stopped applying myself. I never put much effort into my homework, and I only did the bare minimum to scrape by and to maintain the grades I was already getting. Based on the judgment from my teachers (that was part of their job), I perpetuated the cycle.

When I entered university, I maintained this image of myself. I skipped class, I didn't focus on my homework, and I didn't apply myself overall. I was surprised when I ended up on academic probation. This level of application didn't quite have the same B and C results as it had in high school. A letter went home to my parents, and I was mortified. The guidance counselor set up a meeting, and she bluntly told me I needed to change. She said something so profound; she said, "If you keep seeing yourself as somebody that just squeezes by and does the bare minimum, you will forever just squeeze by and do the bare minimum. So what do you want to do here? Do you want to show up as an A student? Or do you want to show up as a B or C student?"

I didn't quite connect with what she was saying at the time, but with my new level of awareness, it makes all the sense in the world. I needed to make a fundamental change because the identity I held had created the routine I engaged in related to school, and it simply wasn't going to work anymore. She helped me to change my identity and to shift the concept that I'd held of myself.

At that moment, I made a new decision: I would reject the current identity and step into a new one. I decided to apply myself. I started going to class, studying for tests, and submitting papers on time. This change led me to getting straight A's, and this continued for the nine remaining years of my formal education. When I put in the work, it changed my identity, both as a student and as a person.

Nothing changed except for the idea I held about myself within my subconscious mind. It shifted the way that I expressed myself. With this, I started to realize that my personality was not predetermined. I could actually do something to change it.

It's important to make the conscious decision to reject external ideas of you and the suggestions of others that are damaging. Now is the time to build your self-concept based on who you <u>actually</u> are and who you <u>actually</u> desire to be. Evolving your understanding in this way can shape your identity moving forward.

As you reprogram your identity, you don't need to switch your beliefs entirely. You can switch the meaning you give to beliefs. Some of these beliefs begin in childhood. For example, when I was bullied as a child, I believed what others were saying about me. Their insults became part of my identity, even though I was building this identity based on the perspectives of others. None of it was true or real; I don't even know if my bullies believed what they were saying.

This was solidified early on and followed me into adulthood. Throughout my life, I was told I was too sensitive. I always saw this sensitivity as a weakness, something I needed to rid myself of.

As a defense mechanism, I began to seek out opposite personality traits and try them on. I wondered what was on the opposite side of sensitivity. What was a new identity I could try? Should I be strong and stoic instead? The less I tried to be sensitive, the more I felt cold-hearted. This filled me with guilt and felt entirely inauthentic. Sensitivity was part of my being. How could I reject it outright when it was an integral part of my personality?

Then I sat and thought, *how can I instead change the way I see being sensitive?* I decided to reframe my sensitivity with positive language: "I'm a very <u>loving</u> person. I'm a <u>caring</u> person. I feel emotions very deeply."

I realized that manifestation is all about emotional regulation. If I'm highly sensitive, that means I can tune into emotions with expert precision and use them to my advantage. This makes manifestation easier and more effective.

Through self-talk and reframing, I changed the concept into something positive. Yes, I was still sensitive, but it wasn't a weakness. It was a way forward.

As you take the practice lessons from this book into your daily life, start using the language of the best of yourself. In this way, you speak your best into being.

Ideally, the language you use considers the state you're in and the self you'd like to actualize.

<blockquote>
I am aware of who I truly am.
I have a desire to become a better version of who I am.
I understand that who I am today is amazing.
</blockquote>

These statements stem from your sense of identity—the way you're defined and how you'd like yourself to shift as you become your best.

How are these changes possible when you feel stagnant?

I have countless clients who come to me wanting more from their life. They might want more time to travel, make more money, experience more fulfilling friendships, have more opportunities to serve others, and have more chances to find a sense of purpose. Whatever it is, they have an overwhelming feeling that there is something bigger and better out there for them. This can feel like discontentment with your current life, even boredom if you will.

While they may not realize it at the moment, they've <u>outgrown</u> their current identity and are ready to shed it to evolve. They are pulled by their spirit to change the way they see themselves instead of staying stuck.

Still, they are often resistant to changing their self-concept. They've clung to their identity for so long, both the good and the bad, so why change it now? They've gotten used to staying in this place. They believe that, even when the way it manifests is mostly negative, everything that comes out must still be authentic. They believe that even a slight tweak in their identity would render their being inauthentic.

It often comes down to this platitude: "I am what I am and that's the way that I am." They are taught that their personality is fixed, unalterable, written in stone. They were born this way, and there's no use in fighting it. It just is what it is.

To approach this lack of awareness, I first get clients to realize where their stubbornness stems from. I give them an opportunity to stop and consider how they see themselves.

I ask them to answer the following as truthfully as possible:

What are the things that I say about myself?

How would I introduce myself?

What are the roles that I play?

What makes me happy?

What makes me upset?

What do I complain about?

What am I grateful for?

When do I feel loved?

When do I feel content? Is it by myself? Is it around other people?

Who am I when I am at my happiest?

When do I feel appreciated?

What motivates me?

How do I want to be?

After this deep dive, they often have an idea of their current identity and an answer that illustrates their self-concept. From there, it is up to them how they use this information moving forward.

Even after receiving my advice, some clients decide to stay in the same place. When change would benefit them, they still won't budge. They come up with various reasons—they're not ready to grow, change could be damaging because they are in a vulnerable state, or it would be more attainable in the following month or year. Others try to change the external or the superficial details instead. They alter their bodies, their homes, their wardrobes—they focus on interior design without actually changing the interior that matters most.

These excuses and deviations stem from a choice. They are choosing to reject new opportunities and a more fulfilling human experience and remain as they are. Sadly, they could live the rest of their lives not realizing what they are giving up. It often takes nearly losing their lives to put this in perspective and to make them wish they'd made different decisions.

Of course, I still understand where they're coming from. Their resistance to meaningful change is natural. When we are about to rise to a new level of consciousness, or when we are growing and expanding in our self-concept, that change can be uncomfortable. It can feel more scary than exciting. After all, it is a massive change to move into new territory and change the emotional conception of oneself that's been ingrained. But it can be easy, if you choose it to be.

As you start to do the internal work, you'll likely imagine moving upward out of your comfort zone. You'll start to think of this next step—the higher frequency of vibration—and you'll feel the unsteadiness of this new space. Meanwhile, the vibration you were on previously feels comfortable and predictable, and it will try to lure you back down. From below, it will call out to you: "It's easier down here. This might not be what you want, but it's safe and recognizable."

Realize that this fear, nervousness, or excitement you feel is a natural part of moving up the ladder and advancing toward higher frequencies of vibration. It is all part of your transformation. Throughout the process, you will get the urge to return to safety. It's a lot like a rubber band. You can stretch it, but at a certain point, it will snap back to where it belongs.

Remember that this resistance is growth. If it's not uncomfortable, it's likely not going to change you.

As you move through this, it helps to avoid language centered on being "scared" or "afraid." This fails to completely capture the experience. When you move to a higher plane, are you really afraid? Maybe you're just uncomfortable? Excited even? Whenever I feel nervous, I frame it as the following: "This exhilaration must mean I'm growing." That way, any change that comes has an air of excitement instead of dread. It's like that moment of pure anxiety before jumping out of an airplane; while terrifying, it's followed by a feeling of absolute freedom.

~~

The process of reframing your identity often involves discovering how much freedom you have and the "concrete" facts that you accepted that can be redefined. Ultimately, it means taking what you perceived as a truth and tweaking it.

Recently, I received a message from a woman who was seeking advice about her relationship. After laying out her life story and her current predicament, she inquired about her narcissistic husband, wondering if she had manifested him. After all, her father was narcissistic and her mother stayed with him her entire life. Did she manifest a similar situation? To state it plainly, I believe she did.

She mentioned that she couldn't leave because she was financially dependent upon him. My response was this: This is only your current truth; it can be adjusted. There is a version of yourself that exists that believes you are not dependent on anyone, today you simply <u>believe</u> you are. This belief is making you stay put; it renders you immobile.

While she was merely seeking advice, I provided a way out. She immediately became empowered.

Likewise, you aren't dependent on your spouse. More generally, you aren't dependent on <u>anybody</u>. You build your own life, your own existence, and your own livelihood. Part of the reason why I believe this is because I grew up with parents who had equal roles. Both made roughly around the same amount of money and worked the same amount of hours. Conversely, there are women who still believe that the man is where the money comes from. The man is the provider and the woman is dependent on their provisions.

This comes down to one's mindset. Part of you believes that you deserve this role as reliant. You believe that you deserve to put up with narcissism and toxicity and abuse because you don't have a path toward your own income or autonomy. You may think that you have no other option and that a man is the only source of security.

If you change yourself and reject this underlying identity, you have freed yourself from the prison that you believe defines your life. Just because you haven't, doesn't mean you can't.

My first book *Becoming the One* charted my journey in building a new concept of myself. It explored my growth as I developed into my new identity, detailing when I became self aware and began to reprogram my subconscious mind.

Despite my emphasis on growth, I believe the real change doesn't happen in the <u>becoming</u>. It happens in the <u>being</u>. It occurs in that realization that you <u>are</u> the one—that you aren't just stuck in an endless state of becoming.

If you are forever becoming, you are never being. Therefore, you will never achieve that identity or self-concept that you wish to embody.

Become self-aware. See your self. Create a new idea or concept of self to think from, feel from, and express from. Just remember that this starts <u>right now</u> at this exact moment. You can wait in the "becoming" holding pattern for eternity, but you won't be moving forward.

To pull from a personal experience regarding being and becoming, I always think about my relationship with alcohol. I started drinking alcohol around the age of 14. I grew up in a family where drinking was a way to unwind and have a good time. It was part of our culture and was seen as casual.

At 39, I was considering the best of myself and what that meant. This got me thinking about health and longevity. My attention shifted to drinking. How did it really make me feel? I quickly realized that drinking didn't actually make me feel better. It made me flushed. It made me tired. It gave me heartburn. I would wake up the next day with brain fog or a headache. Even though I wasn't overdrinking and I didn't have a clear problem with drinking, I was still evaluating the effect it was having on my life and if it was a behavior worth holding onto. Eventually, I identified it as being unproductive. Everything I realized about drinking was directly at odds with being my best. It made me feel worse. Shouldn't everything I do make me feel better?

In January of 2022, I decided to try and quit drinking. During that month, I would actively avoid ordering alcohol at restaurants. Around this time, I spent one weekend with my mom and my girls at the Shangri-La Hotel in downtown Toronto. After a day spent swimming, shopping, and riding the subway, we were surprised with an upgraded room at our hotel. Now placed in the presidential suite, we decided to celebrate by popping complimentary champagne that came with the room.

When we went to the mall afterward, I remember having hot flashes and feeling fatigued. Even after just a glass, I felt ill. This ended up being the last drink I had. Afterwards, I thought to myself: "Why is it that I decided I don't want to drink anymore, but I still end up drinking alcohol when it's sitting in front of me?" I didn't have any self-restraint.

I realized that I had not shifted my identity. I still believed that I was someone who drank <u>that was trying not to drink</u>. I needed to accept a new belief about myself and to alter my identity to someone who does not drink.

I thought of people in my life who didn't drink. My brother immediately came to mind. He hasn't had a drop a day in his life. Part of his identity is being someone who doesn't drink. Others around him accept this and never attempt to pressure him.

Inspired by this, I proclaimed from that moment forward I would be a non-drinker and behave as such. At dinner the next night with friends, I expressed my new identity by <u>being</u> it in that moment, not becoming it. As the drink menu was passed around, I declined without even looking at it, simply stating, "I don't drink alcohol," and opting for a green tea instead.

In that moment, I solidified for the first time my new identity. By saying it out loud, I also solidified this in the minds of others. I haven't had a drink since, nor have I had the desire to drink. There is no part of me that feels like I'm missing out. The reprogramming happened in an instant, and I was able to accept and implement this new belief.

Remember, it doesn't always have to be hard. Once you are in the moment, it can come easy.

If we are forever trying to fix the problem, we are stuck in the problem and not in the solution. Going to the solution and stating a new identity—in my case, "I am a non drinker"—often dismisses the problem.

The same can be said for confidence. If we are forever trying to be more confident, we will forever not have the confidence we desire. You have to <u>be</u> in your confidence, acting it out, not becoming it. Acting confident is a decision; you are building an idea of confidence in your mind and choosing to be it in that moment. When you are in this space, you no longer need affirmations or positive self-talk; you live it. This is the moment you've shifted your consciousness and built a new self-concept.

When building your true identity and doing the internal work, you are using the intellectual plane to reframe what's in the personal mind. Essentially, this reprograms the ego for optimal functionality.

As you unfold, you start to see that things that used to be a challenge are no longer a challenge. You realize that stressors in your life aren't as nerve-racking as you previously made them out to be. Ultimately, you start to see that your experience of this life is based on what you choose to experience in this life. Becoming the best of yourself all comes back to shifting your experience by reimagining your identity.

From there, it's imperative that you use this newfound identity for good and avoid feeding the ego. Instead of becoming self-serving or self-centered, apply your abilities toward the service of others so they can also improve their identity and move toward a place of fulfillment.

CHAPTER 4:
Journal Prompts

Reflect on your awareness of self: Explore the statement, "I'm aware of who I truly am." What does this mean to you? How does this awareness of your authentic self influence your journey toward becoming the best version of yourself? Reflect on moments when you have felt a strong sense of self-awareness and how it has shaped your actions, decisions, and relationships. Consider practices or approaches that can help deepen your self-awareness and understanding.

Embrace your desire for personal growth: Reflect on the statement, "I have the desire to become a better version of who I am instead of someone else." What does this desire mean to you? How does it differ from comparing yourself to others or striving to be someone you're not? Explore specific areas or aspects of your life where you genuinely desire growth and improvement. How can you nurture and channel this desire in a way that aligns with your authentic self and supports your journey of self-actualization?

Embrace self-acceptance and growth simultaneously: Reflect on the statement, "I understand that who I am today isn't necessarily bad." How does this perspective of self-acceptance intersect with your aspirations for personal growth? Explore moments when you have embraced self-acceptance while also striving for self-improvement. How can you maintain a balance between acknowledging your current state and embracing the potential for growth? Reflect on the mindset and language you can cultivate to support both self-acceptance and personal development simultaneously.

CHAPTER **FIVE:**

Faith Expressed in Action

"Success reduced to its lowest and simplest terms is faith expressed in action."
- Robert A. Russell, God Works Through Faith

I don't believe in luck. I instead believe you play an active part in your good fortune. Perhaps it's deciding to believe you are lucky, which then attracts the luck you desire, or perhaps you choose to assume that everything works out for you, and then it does. But to believe that some are just created "lucky" and others aren't, doesn't serve you.

There is an intense realization of freedom when you start to see that everything is caused <u>by</u> you and is <u>for</u> you, both the good and the bad. This outlook is how you start to shape your surroundings in your image and to begin to influence your own reality. Good things happen when you listen to and trust yourself—when you are in the flow of your own life. This flow state happens when you stop forcing and just allow, when you think what you would love instead of what you observe, and when you trust that all you ask for is being delivered. It feels light, it feels easy, it feels effortless, and it's because you have become aligned to who you really are. You are the best of yourself when in this flow state.

To allow yourself to be in this state will likely require an awakening or a higher level of enlightenment than you have experienced before. We are spiritual beings having a human experience, and awakening to this idea will be a pivotal shift for you. The recognition of my oneness allowed me to quantum leap my life, and I believe it's important to discuss in order for you to do the same. I will speak about this in the context of FAITH, so we can all understand how this oneness shows up for me.

I feel fortunate that I can now live from a place of faith, although I am aware there are higher levels of it I have yet to experience. Once I started to really tap into and feel this state of faith, it became easy to maintain and choose faith, especially in times when my outside world was trying to trick me. I experience faith in many ways in my life—in the existence of things, in positive experiences, in myself, in others, in a higher power. Although it took a while to find it, my ability to have faith is part of the reason why I've manifested so much in my life. You will not manifest a thing if you do not have faith in that thing, in yourself, and in the source delivering it to you.

WE ARE *spiritual* BEINGS HAVING A HUMAN *experience*, AND AWAKENING TO THIS IDEA WILL BE A *pivotal shift* FOR YOU.

I know many still struggle with faith. They might not find it as a feeling that bubbles up naturally. For some, their relationship with faith fluctuates over the years as they struggle to maintain it. Others might see their outlook on life as more practical, and they can't find a place for faith in their worldview. While this attitude is understandable, it has drawbacks. It can blind you to certain possibilities that are harder to rationalize yet still hold power.

For years, faith was something that was totally separate from my sense of self. I associated faith with religion and a belief in God or a deity. It was about devotion to something you couldn't exactly prove. Because religion didn't play a large role in my life apart from Sunday school a few times as a kid, this didn't quite resonate with me. This continued into my adult life. After having kids, I remember watching baptisms in church and getting the feeling that it was not real, or that it was a bit foolish. The singing, the ceremony, and the ritual made me feel like I was in a different dimension sometimes. I don't mean to dismiss it entirely, but it was something I hadn't believed in or bought into my life. My lack of understanding made me dismiss its possibility.

It took me a while to see that faith wasn't necessarily about the image of a man with a beard that we placed on a pedestal. It was much more than that. The feeling of faith is more connected to our oneness and our awareness. It is more about finding your own conception of God—or spirit, source, creator—based on your own perception. I had to find my own personal understanding, and within this, I could find my own personal reality. You find what you truly believe. Once you find this, you can live it wholeheartedly and allow yourself to create what you want for you. This understanding allowed me to see that there was an answer to my prayers, that every ask would be answered and that I wasn't alone in the creation process. The realization I did not have to do it alone was such a sense of relief!

Before having faith, I believed that I was being whisked through life against my will, that everything occurred was out of my hands. This passive approach felt natural, even though there were so many things I could change to better my situation. I saw the world as a harsh, rough place where things never really went my way. It was a place where you never know what the future would hold or if everything would come crashing down around you at any moment. I would even say things like, "life is hard," without even realizing that I was asking for that to be my truth simply by saying it.

Part of the problem was that I was programmed to reject having faith. When I imagine the source of my skepticism, my university degrees come to mind. I received a degree in sociology and psychology as well as a master's in nursing science. My time in academia taught me that in order for something to be real or to exist, I needed to see it with my own eyes. I needed a present sense impression. I needed to observe it with my 5 senses for it to be "true." It had to be tangible, rational, or reasonable to be worth consideration. Reality was based around logic and reason; there wasn't room for the abstract or inexplicable.

During my studies, I was a research assistant at Princess Margaret Hospital, and I conducted research with breast cancer survivors. One aspect was social research, so it was qualitative. I wasn't just studying lab reports and tracking numbers; I was collecting subjective data. I gathered and conducted interviews that considered people's lived experiences. Their stories informed our conclusions about the truths surrounding breast cancer survival.

Throughout this study, I needed to see the results and outcomes to believe them. It all followed the scientific method; we needed to observe something in order to form our hypothesis. The clinical trial serves as evidence, and it gave us the data we needed to make a diagnosis or to reach our conclusion. It all revolved around results and the process of proving that something exists. I was so conditioned to believe this approach to life that I never even considered an alternative. At the age of 37, with the decision to start studying myself instead of science, I started to believe in something outside of what I could see. I started to consider my relationship with faith for the first time.

My newfound approach to faith came as a sudden, drastic shift in the way in which I saw the world. It activated when I stopped needing to prove something and just allowed myself to know something, whether or not it was there. I started to believe in what I could not see, and I invested in the immeasurable.

From there, I started reading works by Bob Proctor, Napoleon Hill, and Neville Goddard. As I studied their concepts, I simultaneously started working on my self-concept. I realized that the world was a complete creation of my own consciousness. Suddenly, I realized that everything I expected or assumed would happen ended up happening. My eyes were suddenly wide open. I started to perceive the world as less frightening and chaotic. The danger I used to associate with it was dulled. I became less afraid of what could go wrong or what could happen because I realized that I had control over it.

I will never forget one of my first manifestations involving my health after I tapped into this idea of faith. In 2018, I had undergone a journey of extreme weight loss that led to me fainting 3 to 5 times a week . I lost my driver's license and couldn't be alone with my girls. I had to go on sick leave from being a nurse (which I never returned from; this was a giant leap of faith), and I was feeling the urge to start knowing something different for my future. I really wanted my license back. It was so limiting to live without it. Before, I would have figured there was nothing I could do about it, that it was completely out of my hands. Instead, I thought, *You know what? I'm pretty powerful. I'm going to manifest that my symptoms go away and that I get my driver's license back.*

I gave myself three months to make it happen. I focused on what I wanted. I started to believe that I was healthy. I stopped expecting fainting spells and took my attention away from it completely. I didn't think about it, talk about it, or tell anyone else about it. It was like it didn't exist. I instead visualized being in perfect health and getting my license back, and I celebrated both in advance.

With my new thinking, my new assumptions about my health, and the visualizations of being in perfect health, the fainting stopped completely. My doctor submitted a letter after two months of being faint-free but warned me that it could take months to process. Instead, I held the image and idea in my mind for 3 months, and it ended up being exactly three months. I had asked for my license back by the end of November, and it happened November 29.

This was a huge awakening for me. I had opened my mind to alternate perspectives and ways of existing. I had a desire for more and a willingness to change. This all came from reading and realizing that the feeling of faith is all about your own connection and understanding to create your own reality. It was about seeing that the way you're told how things are might not actually be how they are.

This was my first time <u>thinking, living, and feeling from the end.</u> I had to imagine what I could not perceive (the end result) and think backwards from this place that didn't yet exist in the observable world. What if you can believe it and then see it? This was the shift that changed it all. This involved faith in something new.

For example, if you identify as a procrastinator as we discussed earlier, you have faith in the idea that you will procrastinate on the next paper you need to write, so you will act on that assumption. But isn't it altogether possible that you aren't in fact a procrastinator but maybe you procrastinated a few times more than you would have liked in your life? So what if you had faith that you could in fact be an action taker? If you instead think from the end result and start seeing yourself as someone who gets things done, you will begin to believe this new story, and then you will act in the faith of its assumption. You will soon find that with little to no effort, you take action. The old belief that you are a procrastinator no longer ties you down, and you are free to be what you desire to be. The choice to see something that has never been observed came into fruition. The action taker in you was always there, and you finally brought that version of you out.

Many people try to change their behavior. They use motivation and willpower to temporarily change their habits, and they usually end up back where they started. Changing your identity using faith changes you permanently. It is truly the effortless way in my opinion. When we change the beliefs we think define us, our habits will follow naturally.

One fun tool I have used came from Vishen Lakhiani. He suggests that you ask yourself "lofty questions" from the best of yourself. So, the version of you that has everything you want, that has their goals achieved, and that has instilled the identity changes is the person you ask these lofty questions to. Lofty questions involve you asking from **AFTER** the goal is achieved. For example, *How easy was that quantum leap in my business? Why is my body becoming stronger every day? How fun is it to watch this overflow of money come into my bank account?*

Asking these questions subconsciously programs you to be what you desire to be. You are asking yourself questions from the place where you've reached your "best" instead of from your current position where you haven't yet made it. It is speaking from the identity you wish to reside in and affirming from this best version of yourself while having faith that it will come true.

How do you apply faith to your life and build out your own faith system?

It's easier than you'd think. The experience of faith already exists within you. You exercise it in your everyday life. It doesn't have to be faith in God or faith in the universe, but trust me when I say you have it.

Let me get more specific. We trust that gravity keeps us on the ground, or we wouldn't walk out the front door like we do. We don't have to fully understand it to know it exists. We just believe gravity exists, and we live according to its rules. We put faith in an Uber driver and believe they will take us to our destination safely. We don't sit there wondering if they're going the right way; we put our trust in them. We order from Amazon knowing the package will come.

With parenting, it can feel like an insurmountable challenge. At its most stressful, it feels impossible. Still, you have faith that you'll figure it out and make it happen, or else you wouldn't have had children. Oftentimes, your children have the same faith in you as the parent; they put trust in you that you'll raise them well and keep them out of harm's way. They are born with this faith.

Whether it's something as minor as ordering take-out or something major like putting our life in the hands of a doctor during surgery, we have faith. It keeps us hopeful and optimistic. Without it, life might be too bleak to bear.

At a certain point, you rationalize it this way: "This is the way things are, and things are going to turn out the way I want them to be." Of course, that isn't always the case, but it's better to believe this is true and to go with it.

I've noticed a few things about faith in my journey. What you have faith in will show up in your reality. So while we don't want it, because we have faith in it, we observe it. For example, there are some people who go to a restaurant and their order somehow gets messed up. On the other hand, there are others who go to a restaurant and their order is always perfect. When I sit down at a restaurant, I expect that everything is going to be cooked perfectly, that it's going to be served at the right temperature, that it's going to be the best version of that particular dish. With this approach, my food comes the way I ordered it; it's rare that I experience a bad meal or a mistake in my order.

Ask yourself: Do you have faith in what you want, or do you instead have faith in what you want to not happen? Your answer can shape your reality. We can have faith in the thing we fear the most, which then brings it into reality.

Here's another example from my healthcare days. The number one predictor of falls in seniors wasn't their mobility, their strength, or the amount of clutter in their environment, but their fear of falling. We move according to what we have faith in. To fear falling, to have faith in the fall, literally causes someone to move tentatively and not with confidence; in turn, this causes someone to fall. How interesting!

Imagine a relatively common fear: Someone is too afraid to drive on the highway. Where does this fear really stem from? They have faith in accidents. They have faith that other drivers are reckless. They have faith that something is going to go wrong and that an accident is bound to happen. Instead, you can drive on the highway and have faith that everything will turn out fine. You can tell yourself you're a good driver, that you're far from accident-prone, that people on the road know what they're doing, that the act itself is safe. Lo and behold, you go for a drive that day and nothing happens.

We always have faith in some way or another. It can be optimistic or pessimistic, hopeful or doubtful. What's important is what we have faith in.

How does faith impact the other aspects of being the best of yourself? How does it help us speak something into being?

Faith and manifestation are intertwined, but they are not exactly interchangeable. Instead, faith is one key component of manifestation. Without faith, manifestation isn't possible—well, manifestation of what you desire isn't. You will still manifest more of what you have. Your manifestation magnet is never off, be aware of what the attraction is set to. This is because you will only manifest what you have faith in. Consider it this way: Our thoughts are energy; they are vibrational. They manifest and take shape as they are molded by your mind. On the other hand, faithless thoughts are not powerful and hold no vibration. Therefore, they cannot form. Your lack of belief in them, keeps them futile.

To be clear, the thoughts you do not have faith in are useless. Because the faith remains in the opposite. This is why affirmations may not be working for you. You affirm what you want or believe but never actually have faith in it, so it remains powerless. For example, saying, "I am confident," won't change anything if you still exist as someone who is unconfident. Even if you stand in front of the mirror and repeat it hundreds of times, it won't do much. You would still continue to exist without confidence. It's not as simple as speaking something into being because deep down, you have doubt. You are trying to reprogram your subconscious mind, but you are still focused on your insecurities.

Ironically enough, repeating the phrase "I am confident" just affirms the fact that you are not. You are affirming the opposite and solidifying unwanted beliefs instead. After all, how many confident people you know have to repeat this over and over again to truly feel it?

It is more about believing it then repeating it. It's about having honest faith that what you're saying is really true or about to become true in the future. *What if this is actually true?* has been a great question I ask myself to have more faith in affirmations. According to Florence Schovel Shinn, you don't need to affirm something more than once if you have perfect faith. This is a powerful statement that has really helped me to allow myself to have faith. While repetition will eventually reprogram the belief, which could take years, instant belief with faith = effortless.

This idea of allowing yourself to have faith is a powerful one. What we choose to have faith in is the awareness we should all be seeking. You have faith that you're going to succeed; you could also have faith that you're going to fail. You have faith that you're sick, but you could have faith that you're healthy and will remain that way. You have faith more money is on its way, or you may have faith that it isn't. Being aware of where your faith is directed towards and choosing to direct it the other way is profound. I'll never forget when a private coaching client called me one day and said, "You know, Kathleen, I'm done trying to change my beliefs. I'm just going to have faith instead." She freed herself from the prison she was in the moment she realized she could just choose the direction. Others might also choose to "give it to God" or "trust the universe." These are both statements affirming the choice to have faith.

There again are different levels of faith. What does it mean to have perfect faith? To me, this is strong and unwavering faith, and you could not be convinced otherwise. There is a belief to your core that this is true and you trust it fully. While you may not be at this place yet, this experience exists the more you choose to observe faith. Stop doubting and replace.

Go all out and faith will return the favor.

How do you depart this cycle?

I have taught several classes on growing your faith, and I've focused awareness on projecting your faith on the right things. I often have people follow these steps:

Step 1: Understanding & Self-Awareness

Take a step back to figure out what you have faith in. First, consider your three main complaints in your life. Oftentimes, they are the following:

1. My family dynamic is complex.

2. I have no money.

3. I hate myself or my body.

When these are on your mind, you have faith in them. You are perpetuating what you think is true. Hating your job, complaining about your boss to your friends, and venting about your husband are all ways of increasing your faith in what you don't want. This is a great way to keep these experiences alive.

Having self-awareness about what your problem is or what you complain about the most is the first step in changing your trajectory. Otherwise, you will continue to make the same decisions and maintain the same damaging relationships because you've instilled your faith in them. Ultimately, you have faith in something that you don't want. You are unconsciously committed to being mistreated and having what you would define as a miserable life. You are comfortable there. Even though it is volatile, it is a place where you feel safe.

Whenever you feel lost, remind yourself that you do have faith—you just aren't always aware of it, and it may be placed on something entirely unproductive.

Step 2: Choosing Faith

The choice to have faith is what serves you.

It is so important to make a conscious decision to choose something new to have faith in, such as a loving relationship or a more fulfilling life. Believe that the best version of you is possible. See these challenges and problems in your life as the perfect opportunity to prove the best version of you. Choose to see these opportunities as the best way to prove your faith. See yourself thriving, confident, powerful, and optimistic. See yourself moving boldly in the direction of your dreams and see yourself winning big. You will see this in your reality soon, trust me.

Step 3: Studying Faith

There are several great books and chapters about faith. I have found that the more I read about, think about, and practice feeling it, the more my feeling of faith grows. I remember when I chose to read the faith chapter in *Think & Grow Rich* by Napoleon Hill every day for 30 days. I found myself so caught up in the faith feeling that it felt almost miraculous. Even as you read this chapter, your eyes are focused upon the idea of faith, so reading this multiple times will help whenever you find yourself in doubt.

Step 4: Grow Your Faith Idea and Feeling

Once you establish this new belief, believe in it wholeheartedly. Believe in something outside of yourself. Believe that perfect faith is within you. Practice the feeling. When have you had perfect faith before? When have you simply just trusted? Find that feeling again and choose it over and over again. It will find you again.

CHAPTER 5:
Journal Prompts

Reflect on your belief in personal agency: How does the idea that you are active in your good fortune resonate with you? Have there been instances in your life where you felt a sense of empowerment and influenced positive outcomes through your actions and mindset? Explore specific examples and consider the role of personal agency in shaping your reality.

Explore the connection between self-trust and positive outcomes: Reflect on moments in your life when you trusted yourself and listened to your intuition. How did this trust and alignment with your own inner guidance contribute to positive experiences and outcomes? Conversely, think about instances where a lack of self-trust hindered your progress. How can you cultivate and strengthen your ability to trust yourself deeper?

Cultivate faith in yourself and your journey: Reflect on the concept of faith and its role in your personal growth and spiritual well-being. What does having faith in yourself mean to you? How can you nurture and deepen this faith in your own abilities and path? Consider practical ways to strengthen your belief in your potential and embrace the idea of being a spiritual being with a human experience. How does this perspective shape your understanding of yourself and your world?

CHAPTER **SIX:**

YOUniverse

"My mind is a center of Divine operation. The Divine operation is always for expansion and fuller expression, and this means the production of something beyond what has gone before, something entirely new, not included in the past experience, though proceeding out of it by an orderly sequence of growth. Therefore, since the Divine cannot change its inherent nature, it must operate in the same manner with me; consequently, in my own special world, of which I am the center, it will move forward to produce new conditions, always in advance of any that have gone before."
- Thomas Troward,
The Dore Lectures on Mental Science

Most people do not have the awareness as to how their actions create their world. It seems much easier to say that life is simply up to chance, so you allow yourself to be swept up in it all. The belief that you have a destined life has its limits, and you certainly have no ability to change it. If you wish your life to be more like you want it to be, then wouldn't it make more sense to challenge this belief?

The reason why my life outside of me shifted so radically was because of the personal growth and development that I enacted. It was a transformation that was self-motivated. At first, I thought this change would be largely internal. However, I noticed that the more I became the best of myself, the more my outside world altered. My physical observed world became a direct reflection of what I chose it to be in my psychological (inner) world. This was not by mistake.

Is it that the world outside me changed drastically? Did life outside me suddenly get easier? As I stopped to consider this, I noticed the opposite. In fact, the world seemed to be getting harder to navigate, especially during the pandemic. So what changed? I did.

It is you that makes the change. You are the center of your universe. Everything is created from inside and emanates outward to shape the world around you.

There is a common assumption that the universe is separate from you. We trust the universe, we ask for things from it, we say the universe "aligns." Many will regard it as if it's some enigmatic energy field that either blesses you or doesn't. In actuality, the universe is an extension of your oneness. You are not separate from it but a part of it, and in fact, YOU direct its power.

This is why I prefer the term YOUniverse to describe the universe, because the impact you have on the world around you actually stems from yourself. Synchronistic messages, the flow of life, blessings, answers—when you think the world is sending you signals, remember that it all comes from within you. The YOUniverse you create creates your observed world.

The core of manifestation is that the universe/source/god/creator responds to you. The good, the bad—it all comes back to what you put out into the world. I know this is a controversial belief, but it's vital. The universe does not test you. What you see in your world is a direct reflection of something within your inner world. There's no group of judges actively deciding when it's time for your test and creating obstacles for you to overcome.

Instead, any negativity or challenge that exists in your world is an energetic response to what you are putting out into the world. It responds to the vibrations you emit. You literally get back what you put out. Essentially, it is the law of vibration. Like attracts like. You are building the existence around you that gives you what you want back. You want growth, so God says, "Yes, here is some contrast that you will grow through." You need more money, so our source says, "Yes, here is more. I need money." You don't believe you are worthy of a loving relationship: "Yes, I will send you someone who also does not see your worth, or their own."

Of course, this occurs with positive energy as well as negative. Consider a dysfunctional relationship. Oftentimes, we grow accustomed to toxicity and put up with it because it is part of our routine. On a conscious level, we might even say, "I would love to have a loving, healthy relationship. Wouldn't that be amazing?" We can imagine something joyous that exists outside our current situation, and we want this dearly. Still, the energy we emit keeps us stuck in our dysfunctional relationships. Maybe the energy we put out is that we don't deserve better or that change is too improbable. Maybe we attract people that provide dysfunction in our lives and it feels comfortable. Whatever it is, it keeps us stuck in a detrimental cycle.

The issue lies in what you are subconsciously attracting based on your behavior. You are bringing someone into the dysfunction that is you already. They reflect how you see yourself. The irony is that you get upset with this person who provided exactly what you attracted: dysfunction. The universe has responded by giving you a vibrational match.

How does one break out of this cycle? They make a new choice.

Let's say you make a decision: *From this point forward, I am no longer going to say "yes" to dysfunction.* But we don't want to give the dysfunction more attention, as what we resist will persist, so instead we say "yes" to opportunities and people that provide peace, love, joy, and calmness. When someone enters your life that provides these perks, you allow this to be the new normal.

This transition can often feel awkward, especially if you're accustomed to chaos and conflict. To shift to quiet, cozy, and serene can be jarring. As you settle into this new lifestyle, tell yourself how much better things feel, how your life is less stressful, how your relationships provide less of a strain, how your time is now more productive instead of regressive. Make yourself aware of why this new situation is improved even as it feels less comfortable at first. Allow yourself to let the ease in. I want things to be easy so I allow easy in (this might be a good declaration to guide yourself.)

This shift into a new cycle can also work with money. Money exists in our universe. It is a spiritual idea that humans brought into the physical form. The universe of money responds to you based on your vibrations. If you are in a vibrational state of lack and limitation and you tell the universe you need more money, it responds accordingly. Poverty consciousness has a feeling and attracts, much like prosperity consciousness.

You bring to yourself the exact same experience that you already are instead of the one you desire to be. This is where so many people get it wrong. They exude energy that says, "I don't have enough money and need more," and they are consciously saying, "I want more." Instead, the key is to FEEL more—to be in the energy of abundance. You can feel this with zero dollars in your bank account. Turning to gratitude will help dramatically and take you to your very source of abundance: God. The universe only responds to the energy of lack and limitation that you exude.

As you build out your YOUniverse, it's reflected in your interactions with others. The YOU you show up as influences the world you will see reflected for you.

One example comes from a recent interaction with a client who told me a story about their growth that they noticed. This client decided they wanted to invest in themselves and sign up for a coaching program and mastermind. They approached their spouse to ask for permission. Up until this point, my client was aware that they had not not followed through on things but wanted this time to be different.

Once the client asked her spouse, she began to hear back from him all the reasons why she shouldn't do it, including her lack of follow through. My client stopped listening and had an awareness. This decision needed to be made by herself. She knew her own concerns were literally being echoed back to her. She knew she was asking her spouse knowing he would say no, knowing this was her out. This was her safety in staying in the same place. She knew this was an opportunity to step into who she really wanted to be.

In a sense, she saw her own YOUniverse and the changes that needed to be made. Seeing his concerns reflected back on her was an opportunity for her to become the best of herself. It provided necessary awareness. She saw the version of herself that doesn't follow through or finish what she started. In response, she can reprogram herself to now be the type of person who finishes what they start. She made the decision that at that moment she would sign up and finish the coaching program. She would follow through.

This shift all starts with choosing yourself
first instead of focusing on others.

People often seek advice from me about aspects of their life that are unfulfilling or unhealthy. Their complaints usually involve lackluster relationships, a business that isn't building as fast as they'd like, or a job that leaves them lacking. Oftentimes, their worry is compounded by stress. They grow overwhelmed and grow too busy to set time aside for self-reflection, let alone active change. They want a way out or some advice for shifting their circumstance, but they don't quite know where to begin.

One recurring complaint that is central to their issues is simple yet devastating: they are putting everyone else's needs above their own.

I WANT THINGS TO BE *easy* SO I *allow* EASY IN

So many people get stuck in a cycle where they are boosting up someone else's life and building what <u>they</u> want. In the meantime, they create a life that they aren't excited to sustain.

The solution? Choose yourself and put yourself first. This is an integral part to creating your YOUniverse.

While it may come across this way, this act isn't selfish or egotistical. In many ways, it's the opposite. It stems from the understanding that when you are acting at your best, it influences others around you to become their best. When you become the center of your own universe, you then understand that what happens within you changes everything and everyone outside of you. This includes bettering the lives of others.

Consider child-rearing. If you want to raise your children to be well adjusted, happy, and fulfilled, you yourself need to be that first and foremost. Your kids will follow the habits, patterns, and behaviors you enact. You are their teacher, and you teach through your energy and your actions.

I see a lot of parents trying to teach their kids how to love themselves. Let's consider body positivity for example. We want our young girls to love their bodies, yet they have a mother who is always on a diet, trying to lose weight, calling themselves bad names. Meanwhile, they hate themselves and aren't pausing to put in the necessary work. We can't look in the mirror and critique our hair or our bodies one moment and then turn around and tell our kids how special they are. They can feel the energy you're putting off, and it's unconvincing.

Instead of merely teaching, we need to "be" it. We need to actively live out the epitome of our best as an example for others. Your children, as well as others, will then follow suit as they grow into the best of themselves.

I didn't start quantum leaping my life until I made myself a priority and placed myself first. It took me realizing that there's no shame in wanting to be the best and putting time into myself accordingly. Much of my time was spent studying textbooks, taking courses on how to better my nursing skills, and taking courses on how to market myself as a new entrepreneur, but I had not yet taken a course on me. There is a difference between personal and professional development. I focused all my energy on professional development because that was "normal" to do so, but it took me a while to become aware that mentorship and personal growth programs would allow me to excel. I remember when a leader of mine told me she hired a coach, then another leader told me the same thing. It's like it was a secret, but I quickly came to realize that all the entrepreneurs I looked up to studied themselves and had mentors or coaches. I immediately started to consider how I could really be the missing link. I quit my nursing career and replaced it with an online business, yet was making the same amount of money. Coincidence? Not at all. How I saw myself was a limit; my identity kept me exactly where I was.

It took me saying yes to opportunities I previously dismissed as risky. I reminded myself what I was worthy of: "Yes, I'm worth a $10,000 coaching program. Yes, I deserve to have fresh flowers around the house. Yes, I should buy this bag even if it's expensive because it makes me feel confident." This also includes saying no to what doesn't mesh with your lifestyle or distracts you from the work you're doing on yourself. It's okay to say no to going out if it no longer aligns and instead stay in to journal, to rest, to dream.

The more I started asking for time alone and dedicating time to my awakening, the more I asked others for support. Luckily, my husband at the time was responsive to this and aided me in taking away some of the burden so I could put in the time I needed. He would take the girls to the park for an hour so I could put in some work on myself. At certain times, I wanted my family involved in the experience. Whenever it made sense, I would bring my girls with me to meditate with me. In this way, I folded them into my universe by leading from the front.

When you focus on yourself, you are choosing transformation. You are deciding to become self-aware and spiritually aligned. You are consciously deciding to reprogram your subconscious mind. You are choosing to actively behave in a different way than how you've behaved before.

This growth stems from putting you first and realizing that you are at the center of it all. From there, it's all about enacting your beliefs and translating ideas into action. This is universal law. The law of cause and effect is profound and results in taking radical responsibility for the life you now have, realizing everything was created by you. The cause? Your consciousness. The effect? The world you experience.

When many first learn to manifest, they are taught to create a goal or build out their vision board. But after you've constructed your board, a question arises: *What's next?*

A lot of people don't consider the next move. They imagine the vision board will magically transport them to the life they desire. This can't happen without motivation. If we simply lay out our plans, all we are doing is creating the same vision of ourselves without any semblance of growth, awareness, or development. We can stare at the vision board and imagine a potential new life, but it doesn't mean it will be realized.

Life comes as a transmutation of you. It comes from your consciousness; therefore, you have to align your actions accordingly. The question that must be answered when looking at this vision board and the way of life you desire is, *who do I need to be?* The realization of this life depends entirely upon you being a version of yourself you aren't yet aware of. It's not to say you aren't that version; you just don't know it yet. So, the multi-millionaire version of me was always here. The teacher was always there. The manifestation queen was always there. I just needed to realize her.

When the choice arose between returning to nursing and building out my burgeoning network marketing business, I was both anxious and excited. While I didn't know what was in store, I was overwhelmed by the prospect of doing something that actually brought me joy, purpose, and the possibility of financial stability. After consulting with my partner Chris, I decided to take that risk.

As I took the leap into the deep end, we decided to downsize so that I could quit my nursing career. We sold our house and moved into a place that was half the size. This way, if my business didn't grow, we could still pay off the house on Chris's salary alone.

This plan stemmed from a negative place. I don't work within that area anymore. Now, I exist within the potentiality of what could go <u>right</u>, not what could go <u>wrong</u>. I plan for the happily ever-afters. I live as though everything will work out the way I want it to. I buy into the best case scenario and have faith that it will be fulfilled.

This decision to leave my role as a nurse was a huge shift. I was choosing to be a new Kathleen. Before, I was intrinsically tied to my profession. Being a nurse defined me and informed endless hours of my life. It took me five years to complete my master's degree. I remember turning in my final notice and being met with confusion: "What about all your degrees?" They are actually out in the garage in a box. I haven't looked at them in years. I understand now what those really are—just pieces of paper with my name in a beautiful frame that told me that I knew enough, that I'd studied enough, that I was worth enough, that I was capable, that I could finally be considered "good."

I don't need that now.

It took a long time for me to step into this space. Before, I was shooting negativity and doubt out into the universe and, unsurprisingly, having the same handed back to me. Now, I am a woman who is fearless and unstoppable and powerful. It all goes back to belief. I believed in myself enough to attract my current wealth and success. This didn't just happen. I made a conscious decision to go within, to know myself more and to change the way in which I saw myself. I used to identify as shy; I'm not sure where that even came from, but I can see now how I certainly am not shy. I'm actually quite outgoing and social. However, I am introverted, loving my alone time to recharge.

I am the product of what's possible. Still, your success lies in your hands. Me believing in your success means nothing. You believing in it means everything. Be honest with what you want to step into your purpose and create your YOUniverse.

Just remember: while it is your YOUniverse, others can still add to it. They can reflect aspects of yourself to give you insight and perspective. Funnily enough, those who trigger you the most are often the greatest teachers. After all, they are teaching you about you. Relationships are reflections, and their goal is to help you grow. Every person is there to teach you something about you, and when you take this responsibility, you stop asking why others are wrong. You look within to ask, "Why do I accept this type of person instead?"

Your YOUniverse is composed of many things, creating a complex pattern and program of creation. These include the concept you hold of yourself, the emotional conception of yourself (the feeling of YOU), the way in which you self-express, the actions you do or do not take, your perception and perspective of the observable word, your choice and perception of relationships, your spirituality/presence/oneness, and how often you are in your personal mind (take things personal).

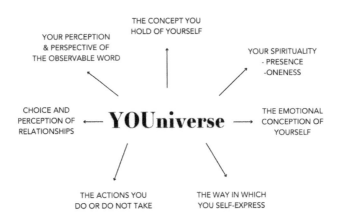

CHAPTER 6:
Journal Prompts

Reflect on your perception of the universe: How do you currently view and understand the relationship between yourself and the universe? Do you tend to see the universe as separate from your own being or as an extension of your oneness? How does this perception shape your experiences and interactions with the world around you? Explore specific instances where you have felt a sense of alignment or synchronicity, and reflect on how these experiences may be connected to your own internal state.

Explore the concept of the YOUniverse: How does the term *YOUniverse* resonate with you? Reflect on the idea that the impact you have on the world stems from within yourself. How does this shift in perspective empower you to take responsibility for your experiences and influence your reality? Consider specific examples where you have witnessed the power of your thoughts, beliefs, or actions shaping your external circumstances.

Deepen your understanding of inner guidance: Reflect on moments when you have received synchronistic messages, experienced the flow of life, or felt blessed or answered. How can you further cultivate your ability to recognize and trust these signals that originate from within yourself? What practices or approaches can you adopt to strengthen your connection to your inner guidance and intuition? Explore the ways in which this deepened understanding of the YOUniverse can enhance your personal growth and overall well-being.

CHAPTER **SEVEN:**

Oneness Vs. Separatism

When I started to study manifestation during my adulthood, I slowly began to believe in something bigger than was outside myself and my physical body. I started to have faith in the universe and whatever that entailed. I don't know what exactly I started to believe in but the word universe felt "believable". Was I simply in awe of the vastness of space and the stars and planets? Did I believe in the universe as a powerful field of energy? It was hard to grasp exactly what I was directing my faith toward because the universe remained an enigma. Whatever it was, I experienced existential humility when considering the immensity of the universe and seemingly how small and insignificant I was in comparison.

However, it dawned on me that I wasn't insignificant in the face of the universe. Instead, I began to believe that I was <u>one</u> with the universe. The universe was not in fact separate from me, but I was instead a part of it and was therefore able to influence it.

It was this pursuit to understand the universe that led me to explore the concepts of oneness and separatism and how they affected my ability to manifest. My later understanding would shift to identify this entity, this energy, this guidance, as God.

Before we explore my definition of oneness, let's first consider what I mean when I mention God.

Throughout this book, I am sharing my personal understanding of God. When I say God or Creator/Source/Spirit, this is simply the language I use to discuss spirituality. While I used to label it as the universe, these terms now feel more fitting.

Before, I didn't feel comfortable using the word God. You might be in that same headspace or use another term entirely; this is absolutely okay. I understand that belief differs from person to person. There's power in considering spirituality from various perspectives. When I use the word *God*, my goal is not to enforce any belief set. Instead, I implore you to find what spirituality means to you and to use the language that feels most natural.

With that in mind, what is oneness?

Put simply, oneness is when you are working with the universe or with your concept of God instead of keeping yourself and your spirit separate. In this situation, God or the universe is working through you. You essentially become a vessel for your spirituality.

How do you know when you are in touch with your oneness? It's often a feeling of deeper connection. You dip into a flow state where you are at your best and in touch with your spirit. Everything feels easy and effortless. You are able to pull energy from both the feminine and the masculine. You exist in a space where you feel inspired. You are able to take action without feeling like you're forcing anything to happen.

The experience of flow state puts you in touch with your intuition. This "gut feeling" is guided by God; it exists as an extension of your oneness and your connection.

For me, this deeper spiritual connection is a different approach to prayer. Through my oneness, I am in contact with God all day without engaging in the actual act of prayer. Through the simple act of sharing my emotions and feeling gratitude for the life I live, I am praying. This in turn creates more things to be grateful for. I am aware that my thoughts are my asks or my prayers.

Any desire that moves through me within this state is a result of my oneness. But it doesn't just stop with me. I can also fulfill the wants of others and help them attain a better life alongside myself, through my teachings. This is doing God's work, or answering the call to good.

Essentially, I am defining a state of being that allows you to feel one with, supported by, and co-creating with a life force that allows you to be your most powerful self.

On the opposite end of the spectrum is separatism—the belief that your spirituality is separate from yourself. This belief would maintain that you and the universe are separate, that you and your life are separate, that you and the god of your understanding are separate.

From this perspective, the universe does not work through you. It is instead something out of your reach that you are unable to properly harness.

If you believe you exist separate from God, then you aren't fully aware of your power. You trust that someone or something else is going to provide for you as well as take away from you. You have something to praise for your good fortune as well as something to reject if life doesn't sway in your favor. If there is negativity in your life and you feel a separation from God, you may curse Him: "Why did you do this to me?" With this mindset, it is easy to feel forsaken. If things are really unfortunate, you may even feel abandoned.

When you're separated from your spirituality, there's no interconnectedness. When you want to interact with God, you have to speak to God as if He is separate from you. You are asking for something outside of you instead of channeling something that is already working through you. In this sense, separatism can be less effective.

Your understanding of God, whether it is your oneness with God or your separation from God, influences your ability to manifest. I reached this conclusion through personal experience and the exploration of my spirituality.

As I became more inquisitive about the world in relation to my oneness, I noticed the magic happening. I would think something and the universe would respond to the unfolding of it. One early example sticks out in particular. I wrote down on a piece of paper that I would love to be on television. I wrote it down, unattached to the outcome, curious if I could manifest it. A week and a half later, I was introduced to someone who asked me to have a makeover on a TV show.

I tested this further, saying, "I'd love to have a coffee today." The next thing I knew, someone showed up at my door with a coffee that I hadn't asked them for. This expanded beyond simple tasks as I began to ask for money. Lo and behold, I manifested exactly $21,795 in my bank account, the exact number I had written down. I started to realize that the universe could work in my favor instead of as an entity I had no control over.

I started to practice letting my oneness speak through me so I could reach a consistent flow state. This not only aided my personal life, but it also benefited my coaching career. I recently put together a three-day live event called "Riches." I was so much in my spirit, I don't even remember what I said over the course of those three days. I wasn't working off any notes whatsoever. I simply spoke and saw how impactful it was for the audience. In these moments, I was fully in my oneness. The messages came through me, the information and knowledge stored in the universe to be relayed through me for those needing to hear it. Most of my teachings end up this way. Most people say that I taught exactly what they needed to hear. My response: *Yes, God asked me to teach on this.* I didn't hear a voice in my head telling me to specifically teach on this, but I followed a nudge, a thought that said, this week I should teach on this. It never fails or falters.

How does all this happen if there isn't something other than myself speaking it into existence? How are these situations created if there isn't some source of higher power? Is there some energy field or formless substance more powerful than yourself?

As I experienced the influence of my oneness more and more, it became abundantly clear. The information we share—whether it's a speech, a book, a study—all comes from one place: God. While it's shared by the human as a vessel, it originates in this formless substance.

Before my awakening, I would have believed the source of my abundance and success was the universe providing. I would have deduced that it was simply my wants and the universe aligning in some way. I would have used the language of coincidence to describe the phenomena and prided myself on being more practical. This perspective even exists in my first book *Becoming the One.* In my stories involving money, falling in love with my body image, and becoming more confident, I considered the universe's role in my good fortune as separate from my own. I didn't consider my impact as much.

This was my understanding up until the launch of *Becoming the One.* I had written all about reprogramming my concept of self to become my best and laid out my journey and how I became a more prosperous version of myself. Still, I had several blind spots – I needed to experience more growth surrounding faith and my concept of God.

I was lucky enough to get Bob Proctor to write the foreword for the book. During a live mastermind call with Bob and several other people, someone inquired, "What is God's role in manifestation? Where does God come in during the process?" Bob's rebuttal was that we are one with God. As one recognizes their oneness with God, their magic and their power begins to unfold. He insisted that the power that God has to create also exists within you and works through you. He even spoke to the idea that God didn't create us in his image but that we created him in ours. This resonated with me deeply. My understanding of God is not a man, but an energy and a lifeforce that we may never get to "see" with our eyes. It may be out of this realm of awareness for us in this reality. But then Bob said something that hit me.

Bob continued: "If you want to read a story about someone becoming one with God, read Kathleen Cameron's *Becoming the One*." His comment blindsided me. At first, I rejected this. My book wasn't about God. But after a few minutes, I let what he said sink in and saw the significance of his words. I began to cry.

I realized that my awakening that was central to my current success was the moment when I found God. I found the god of my understanding; it was my own interpretation based on my lived experience. From then on, I had a clearer understanding of my relationship with faith.

What happens when this sense of oneness wavers? What about those days when it's harder to tap into your faith and exercise your spirituality?

We all experience doubt. We encounter days when it's much harder to make things click. It could be a fogginess or frustration that obscures our ability to tap into our spirituality. It could be that we're finding it harder to manifest what we want. Whatever it is, it feels like a blockage that we don't quite know how to address.

Do I feel a connection with God to the fullest extent every day? No. Do I know that it's still there even when it's a struggle to find it? Yes.

During my low points, I never believe that I am entirely disconnected from God. There's never a moment when I consider myself fully separated. Instead, I just consider these as times when I don't feel the oneness as much as I usually do.

The same goes for you. While we may or may not be tuned into our oneness at any given time, oneness is still always present and accessible. You are always one. You are always connected in some way. The goal is to then feel your oneness as much as you possibly can. Personally, I feel this the most when I'm open and I'm functioning as a channel. In this state, God is flowing to and through me.

Despite this connection remaining open regardless of circumstance, one can switch off their oneness simply by turning their back to it.

There are many reasons behind this rejection. It could stem from one's lack of recognition, a lack of belief, or a lack of awareness regarding their oneness. Some might not realize that oneness is the aim, let alone ways to achieve it. They might be misinformed or haven't put in the work. They may not want to tap into their oneness, even after it is offered to them.

When it comes to spirituality, people exist on a spectrum of awakening and awareness. Some are aware and in touch with their oneness, some are completely unaware, and others are still stuck in the Matrix. Some reject that there is any additional force helping them on their journey. Others dismiss their oneness out of fear or an absence of love.

The problem with this is that the God in all of us is experienced through love. Any time you are in fear instead of love, you exist outside of your oneness and instead reside in your <u>humanness</u>. In this state, you exist separate from your spirituality and are grounded by the confines of the human body. You are limited by the physical plane. Essentially, this moves you away from your loving state. We are spiritual beings having a human experience, but sometimes we forget this and get very good at believing we are human. Others are seeking a spiritual experience for their human, which keeps you believing you go in and out of your spirit, instead of being that spirit itself.

Once you are shut off from the spiritual, it's just the human part of you running the show. You exist entirely in your mind and body. You end up going through the motions and believe destiny is out of your hands entirely. You invent programs built around your own thought patterns without any divine influence. You reject the incredible power that you possess. Within this state of humanness, any action becomes much harder. You feel like you need to put forward extra effort to achieve the same results. Without the spirit involved, it becomes a slog to achieve anything.

It takes remembering who you are and what you're made of to tune into the spiritual and rebuild your relationship with God. From there, it's about finding a balance between understanding that we have spiritual awareness as we work as vessels and that we are also having a human experience. Connecting back to spirituality is always the answer and often requires you to stop focusing so much on what you observe.

Coming to terms with my oneness has allowed me to become a powerful manifestor. I am confident that the force of God is within me and working through me.

Despite my advice, it is <u>your</u> personal understanding of God that creates your results and your success. I don't want you to believe what I believe. My job isn't to convince you that you're one with God or that you're separate. My aim is instead to present multiple perspectives.

I want you to develop your own beliefs surrounding God to guide you on your journey. Whatever belief serves you and empowers you is the belief to follow.

To assess where you currently exist regarding your relationship with God, I want you to step outside of the box and see your beliefs from a new perspective.

Consider the following:

Do you believe in anything at all? In other words, do you believe in something outside of yourself? Do you believe that this something is a higher power?

Do you believe that there is some force guiding you? Describe this force. Is it formless? Is there an image attached to it? What do you call this source or higher power?

Do you believe that this force or energy can only be accessed if you are a good person? Do you believe that if you are bad or evil, this energy is inaccessible?

If you do believe, are you one with a god or deity? Do you believe you are an extension of that god and that their source power moves through you? Or do you instead believe you are separate from it?

If you feel <u>separate from</u>, are there any experiences from your life that have taught you that you could be <u>one with</u>?

Your answers provide a helpful starting point. They create a platform to then build your belief. From there, it's about developing your own understanding and applying it to your life.

One thing to realize is that you have access to God at any time no matter what. It's not dependent on if you are good or bad. It's not about accessing it only if you're worthy of it or deserve or only if you spread the word of God. It exists despite your belief.

Over the course of my coaching career, people have come to me who believe in absolutely nothing outside of themselves. They feel as though there is nothing besides their body. They are devoid of soul and spirituality and see this as the most practical approach.

On the other hand, I have those who come to me from organized religion that have been led by certain beliefs and understandings that shaped their upbringing and provided a rigid set of moral standards to abide by.

My advice to both is the same: Ignore the idea of God you were exposed to. Instead, build God in your own image.

I now see organized religion as a way for humans to categorize and conceptualize the chaos of the universe. It's an attempt to understand and resonate with God instead of accepting the trueness and totality of what God really is. After all, the idea of God is easier to digest if we're all imagining the same thing. Still, God is so much more than that. He's not a concept you can sum up with a simple image. He doesn't take human form. He's an entity or energy. In this way, God is not the "other." He doesn't judge. He simply accepts. He doesn't see us as flawed. On the contrary, he made sure we were divinely made. After all, do you really think God would create something he's not proud of?

So many of us desire to have faith in God or a higher power. We hope that someone or something is going to deliver for us, care for us, support us in times of strife or suffering. We have faith that we get to exist in the afterlife, that our mortal life isn't exactly the end. Oftentimes, we blindly deliver these hopes into the universe, wishing for them to come true without our direct input or action.

Through our oneness, we should instead tap into the faith of God, not just to have faith in God. If we recognize that God works through us and we are enacting his work, then we don't necessarily need to have faith in God. Instead, we need to have the same kind of faith that God has in his own abilities. God doesn't doubt his ability to create. God isn't experiencing insecurity about his physical body. God doesn't question whether he is good enough. If God doesn't, then why should we?

For some reason, we separate ourselves from the divinity within us by telling ourselves that we're not good enough. Once we tap into our oneness, we can harness the confidence of God as it flows through us.

Once we *tap* INTO OUR *oneness*, WE CAN HARNESS THE CONFIDENCE OF *God* AS IT FLOWS THROUGH US.

Being closer to the source of your oneness isn't a solitary spiritual experience. It has the ability to activate a change in our collective consciousness. If we are all in touch with our oneness, we are one step closer to fixing what ails us. Suddenly, issues such as famine, poverty, crime, and war are much more manageable.

Unfortunately, most people have yet to reach this place. They aren't entirely in touch with their sense of self or their relationship with God, and they are unable to harness this potential. Furthermore, they haven't activated their ego and aligned it with their spirit. What if you are divinely made, and the moment you connect with who you really are your power sets in? This has been my experience and the experience of hundreds of people in my community.

CHAPTER 7:
Journal Prompts

Reflect on your realization of oneness with the universe: Describe a specific moment or realization when you shifted your perspective from feeling insignificant to recognizing your connection with the universe. How did this shift in belief empower you to see yourself as a participant in the manifestation process? Reflect on the ways in which this understanding has influenced your ability to shape and influence your reality.

Explore the impact of oneness versus separatism: Reflect on your journey of exploring the concepts of oneness and separatism concerning your spirituality and ability to manifest. How has the belief in oneness enhanced your sense of empowerment and connection with the universe? Conversely, how has separatism limited your belief in your own ability to harness the power of the universe? Consider specific examples and experiences that highlight the effects of these perspectives on your manifestation journey.

Cultivate a sense of interconnectedness and empowerment: Reflect on practical ways to foster a deeper sense of oneness with the universe and your ability to manifest. How can you integrate the belief that the universe works through you and that you are an active participant in the manifestation process? Explore practices such as mindfulness, meditation, or affirmations that can help strengthen your connection and alignment with the universe. How can this shift in perspective positively impact your manifestation abilities and overall sense of well-being?

CHAPTER **EIGHT:**

Ego and Spirit

Within our society, the ego is often vilified. It's seen as a toxin that you should purge for the sake of being a better person. The belief is that this absence of ego brings you closer to your spirit and helps you achieve oneness.

I instead believe that the ego is necessary for success. It is needed to lead us, to help us grow, to remind us of our aspirations, to put our purpose and desires into action. Essentially, your ego pushes you to be the best of yourself.

Consider it this way: your ego is what wants to win. The ego is what wants to be seen. The ego is what wants more money, more success, more recognition. In this way, the ego provides motivation and drive because it is always repeating, "I'm not satisfied." Being dissatisfied is not necessarily a bad thing; it can be positive. It keeps you on the creative plane. It means you have an innate desire for more and you strive for it. This is all a necessary aspect of the ego.

What built my 20-million-dollar business? My ego. It drove me to achieve more and led me to where I am now. My business wouldn't be the success it is now if I didn't follow my calling and my ego didn't build it.

When I was first starting out with my business, I made a decision to focus on me. I joined a course, I started studying every day, I sought help. While this seems self-centered on the surface, I made it about me to change the lives of others for the better. I upgraded my family's life by changing my view of myself first. After years of coaching, the focus has become other people and shifted away from my needs.

Ego can lead you to the place you'd rather be. It is especially helpful when you are launching a new project or pursuing a new career. You need to prove yourself, or have confidence, or believe in yourself. Somebody has to talk you up, so why not make it yourself?

When harnessed and explored in a healthy way, there's a purpose for your ego. It just needs to be kept under control. As long as you recognize this part of you and keep it centered, the ego can become an immensely powerful tool. All the while, consider the intentionality of your ego. Are you using it for a useful or positive aim?

It all starts with reframing the belief that the ego is negative. To do this, it helps to understand what the ego is and how it relates to the spirit.

How do we define the ego?

I consider the ego as a subset of the personal mind. It exists on the intellectual place, is part of your mind and thus part of your human. Your ego exists in your human; in contrast, the spirit exists regardless of the human or not. I even refer to my ego as my "human." Essentially, the ego is what makes a situation about you. It focuses on the self. It's the part of you that takes everything personally: *My feelings were hurt. My perspectives weren't considered. My needs weren't met.* When you are with your ego, you make a deliberate decision to have a situation reflect on your being, your actions, your will, your existence.

While this reaction is often interpreted as self-serving, it can also be considered productive. After all, if you don't make a situation about yourself to some extent, how do you get anything substantial accomplished? At a certain point, you have to say, "I want this life. I want this success. I want this money." Otherwise, there is no source for your motivation. You aren't in the headspace to help yourself, let alone others. As long as your ego is healthy and well-balanced, this focus on the self is motivating.

On the other side is the spirit, which is awareness. Spirit's language is through feeling. Unlike the ego, the spirit does not have thoughts; however, it is <u>aware</u> of your thoughts. In spirit, you're so connected to your oneness that your personal mind has fallen backward and awareness has come forward. When you are in your spirit, there's less of a reliance on reasoning and thinking. In this space, you aren't trying to rationalize. Instead, you're making decisions based on pure intuition.

It is when the ego and spirit work in tandem that the best of yourself can be achieved.

While my ego was the drive and motivation for my successful coaching business, my spirit is what made the journey so fulfilling. Connecting to the sources of it all allowed me to be in a state of ease and flow and absolute faith.

There is always a dichotomy in life. Nothing exists in isolation; everything exists in opposition. At different ends of the spectrum, there is alignment and correlation between all these dichotomies.

It is how much you are in your soul versus in your mind. When you are more in your ego you are less aware of your oneness, and thus not allowing the universe to flow and be used by you as much than if you are in your spirit more. After all, does God have an ego? No because there is no mind present. This balance between the two is key as they cannot be without one another.

I often compare this complementary relationship to the relationship between masculine and feminine energy or the spiritual versus the mechanical. As you consider the two, you realize that there are two ways of functioning.

When you are in the <u>mechanical</u> of life, you are accomplishing duties, going through the motions, fully involved in the hustle and grind. If you instead allow yourself to be <u>in spirit</u> first—to be attuned with who you are, to connect with your purpose, your calling, your mission—then the mechanical action you take every day will be far more powerful. Ideally, you have the spirit and mechanical combined.

The ego and spirit works in similar ways; they are both invaluable and more powerful together. The ego is necessary because you can't create without it. As the ego builds, it assists the spirit. Still, the ego needs to be kept under control and balanced with the spirit. This careful balance defines the dichotomy. Without it, the ego can easily overtake the spirit by introducing insecurity and rationale into the equation. Essentially, the human part of you can harm the spirit.

The ego serves as a filter for the spirit and can stop you from expressing yourself. As the spirit flows through you undisturbed and unabashed, the ego stops certain thoughts and questions truths that you've accepted. "I don't know if people are going to like what I'm about to say. I don't know if this is true. I don't know if this definition is the most accurate." This hesitation suppresses the spirit. In this instance, you move out of the spiritual plane completely by allowing your reasoning mind to judge and second-guess your spirit. Oftentimes, the ego deems these thoughts as not good enough because it makes it about you and the way that others perceive you. In this moment, you move from being in flow to existing on the intellectual plane.

This is where the ego resides. It's that voice in your head that's never content, telling you that you should be more, you should do more, you should have more. It tells you that you should care what others think about you. That you should have a nicer car, a bigger house, a more fulfilling job. This not only limits our beliefs, but urges you to compete with others and compare yourselves to them. This can stem from a place of insecurity. People may tell you that you're "less than," and you want revenge: "I'm going to be better than you. I'm going to get this job over you." This is usually an attempt to overcome the wound that was created when other people put you down.

In contrast, the spirit understands that there is an infinite supply of wealth and abundance available. Despite what the ego says, it's not finite. The irony is that the ego motivates us to tap into that abundance and prosperity, even though it's our spirit informing us that it exists. It's important to keep in mind when our ego gets in the way and limits our potential.

Let's say that you have a job that involves recognition for performance. Someone is arguing with you about who should get the recognition for the job well done. In your eyes, you aren't getting a fair share. They are asking you to engage in an argument and state that you don't deserve the sole recognition. At this moment, you are in your ego, trying to prove your worth. You believe the recognition is a direct reflection of the time or energy that you put in. Because of this, you will fight tooth and nail for the "right" amount.

In contrast, the spirit would say, "Yeah, sure, let's split the recognition!." This is because you know you will be divinely compensated somewhere else. In the example above, you put your spirit aside and allowed your ego to come forward. In your spirit, you instead realize that you are being compensated for how many people you help in totality throughout the course of your life. In this instance, you are deciding between an ego response or a spirit response.

In the way I present it, the spirit may sound healthier. It is the highest level of awareness where the outside world doesn't influence you; it just is. So why don't I allow myself to stay entirely in my spirit? Isn't true enlightenment the ideal? Isn't that nirvana? Wouldn't that be my personal utopia?

It's because I have a mission to fulfill here in the service of others. I have a purpose in mind for my human experience. To fulfill my job, I need to combine a higher level of awareness while still utilizing my ego.

I could live in the middle of nowhere and lead a simple life and be "enlightened" without pursuing my ego. I could experience a heightened level of awareness—true mastery, true enlightenment—without caring for money or material things. But the ego moves me to desire more, the pursuit of helping others. I become the best of myself through helping others to do the same. And my human experience has value, is important and I'm here to receive it all.

Despite the benefits mentioned above, a lot of suffering sits in the ego. It has the ability to be detrimental and damaging if it gets out of hand. When you are working from your ego exclusively, you make it so much about you that you lose things to be grateful for in your life. You stop focusing on available areas of improvement. You might feel you've failed in some way. Whatever the case may be, the more you move into your ego, the further you get from your spirit. The ego asks, "What did I do wrong? Why don't they like me? Why do bad things keep happening to me?"

I see this time and time again in business. Many of my clients are entrepreneurs. When they enter my world, instead of focusing on their desire to build a successful business, they lean heavily into their ego and decide they aren't good enough or worthy of success because they haven't yet achieved the success they set out to do. Their mind tells them, "You don't know enough. You don't make enough money. You've failed. How could you possibly help anyone else?" At this moment, they exist in a place of comparison and very much in the gap of their desired outcome. It is my duty to help them realize that what the ego is saying about themselves simply isn't true. I help them to see that spirit is where happiness, joy, fulfillment lies. The more you love yourself for who you are, the less the ego will interfere. Just because it hasn't happened yet does not mean it can't be done. The past does not indicate the future unless you believe it does.

I try to stay out of my ego as much as I can. Still, I can't help but notice it. Fortunately, I can see when it's a productive use of the ego and when it's unproductive.

Any time you take something personally, your ego is functioning in an unproductive way. For example, a friend tells you that they're not up for going out that night. They're tired and not in the proper headspace. Instead of simply accepting their reasoning and understanding where they're coming from, you make it about you. In your ego, it must mean that they don't want to spend time with you. It must mean you're not good enough. It must mean they don't like you.

The ego has told you a story that's not necessarily based on any truth. Based on that story, you will start to sabotage that friendship. Reframing can help you by saying to yourself, "I guess it wasn't meant to be," or, "I'm glad they are taking care of themselves."

Ego, especially when it's coupled with superiority, has the power to disintegrate your sense of self. Fame, for example, can become detrimental when you buy into what the ego is telling you and how the world defines you. By society's definition, your fame makes you above everyone else. You're a star, and the world has told you this over and over again. While this is a construct, it's easy to believe when it's constantly reflected back at you. In this state, it's easy to be consumed by your ego. It's easy to love yourself so much that you start to believe that you might be better, even if you're not aware of it. It's easy to place yourself on a pedestal and consider yourself superior to everyone else. One thing Bob Proctor always told me was to take him off the pedestal; no one is better than anyone. I truly believe we are all the same, and this has helped me to love myself more and give others more grace and compassion when they don't love themselves.

Instead, frame your fame or influence as the following: "I'm so grateful for this platform to help influence others positively." If you are well-known or powerful, using your platform for good will bring you closer to your spirit and allow you to fully live in your purpose and/or calling.

THE MORE
YOU LOVE
yourself
FOR WHO YOU
ARE, THE LESS
THE EGO WILL
interfere.

Of course, we want people to love themselves, but when is loving yourself exercising too much of your ego? Can you love yourself too much? We have heard people say, "They have a big head," or, "They are full of themselves." What I have found is that oftentimes when we describe these things, we are often referring to someone who actually doesn't love themselves but wants everyone to think they do. Or, the self-love has turned into believing they are in fact "better" than someone else. But I do not believe it is possible to love yourself "too much." Self-love is simply expressing a favorable emotion towards oneself. Having an empowering viewpoint of yourself is our natural state. So, if you're too careful or meek when expressing your ego, this limits your self-love. We're so scared that we will like ourselves too much (or that people think we do). We believe that this self-perspective is actively damaging. It's all about keeping yourself in check and making sure it doesn't get out of hand. I do think I'm an amazing woman, but I don't believe I'm better than anyone. It's about remaining humble, remaining in service to others, all while seeing yourself in a positive light.

At the other extreme, your own mind can create so much negativity and self-loathing. The mind is a very powerful thing; the more you tell it a sad story, the more you tell it that you're not worthy enough, the more you lose sight of the incredible life that exists right in front of you.

We are often scared of liking ourselves. For many years, I lived that. As a kid, I was often told that I was less than and I felt it. I believed I was too flawed to assert my ego, that it was better to accept my fate and stay silent. I truly believed I was less than, and I continued to keep that program going. Although I didn't like it, it was comfortable and what I was used to.

At a certain point though, I began to overcompensate. I used my ego to reprogram myself and reject my insecurities. I became inspired by the insults. I thought I was less, so I worked harder to achieve more. In trying to prove myself and push my ego, I ultimately transformed for the better.

Now, I know that these insults aren't true. I've since established genuine confidence in myself, and this helps keep my ego in check. Now that I've achieved what I wanted, I don't need my ego to motivate me as much. But it helped me for the better. This was a positive use of my ego. Because I felt flawed, I wanted to prove myself. Good thing I chose more personal growth and development because I have since moved out of this need. I do what I do now for the joy of it, and not about "proving" myself. But this energy can be motivating, and can help you get unstuck if you need it.

I had someone ask me once, "Are you teaching people how to be delusional?" I thought this question was funny, and I answered enthusiastically, "Absolutely!."

The dictionary defines delusional as such: "Characterized by or holding false beliefs or judgments about external reality that are held despite incontrovertible evidence to the contrary."

Often, we are delusional about who we are. We have let our personal mind tell us because people don't like us, we aren't good enough. Because we didn't get all straight A's, we are stupid. Because we aren't thin and beautiful, we aren't going to ever be successful. The evidence to the contrary is societal norms and values that aren't real unless we make them our reality by believing them.

So yes, we will create a new delusional view of ourselves with a healthy use of our ego and love the heck out of ourselves until we change the world.

There are both dark and light sides of the ego, and it can help or harm your journey. You just have to be careful to ensure that your ego doesn't take over and send you spiraling. It's about finding a balance between a healthy use of the ego to advance you, and being in a state of spirit and oneness and flow to stay grounded and open.

The ego and the spirit are invaluable. The problem is that the ego works at the same time as spirit but in opposition. Their potential is discovered when striking a balance between the two and finding some semblance of harmony.

This is when you become the most powerful. It allows you to transcend beyond the average human experience.

This starts with identifying and understanding the ways in which you express your ego, including when you are over-reliant on your ego and should be more in touch with your spirit.

Ask yourself about when you are in your ego. When are you in your ego in a damaging way? How about in a constructive way?

If you often find that your ego is damaging, consider when the following situations apply:

When do I make a situation about me?
When do I feel that my feelings are hurt?
When am I judging others?
When am I criticizing others?
When am I blaming others instead of myself?

As you reflect on your ego, you may replay past experiences or recall behaviors of yours that were damaging. You might remember moments that were highly emotional or traumatic. This all works to program the subconscious mind. A moment where you felt overwhelming embarrassment, guilt, or shame is stored so that it can be re-lived and re-experienced. It defines your self and your ego as you move forward, creating doubt, anxiety, and insecurity.

What's buried in the subconscious mind will manifest in the physical plane whether it's true or false. The subconscious doesn't know if you are replaying a memory, experiencing an observed state in the present, or if you are imagining something; it believes it. So, by replaying negative experiences, you're reprogramming your subconscious mind with it and making it more real.

Luckily, this can be addressed when reframing the memory. Return to the source of that trauma and re-experience it without the experience that you had. Delete the negativity you felt from the memory. Create a new experience, downplay the emotional part of it, tell yourself a new story about what happened, even revise the day and imagine the outcome you would have loved to have had instead. We often tell ourselves what we would have done "next time," so imagine that now! This is a highly beneficial manifestation technique from one of my favorite authors, Neville Goddard.

If this isn't possible for you, at least try to become neutral toward the memory. Give yourself the grace to move past any perceived wrongdoings. You may have acted entirely from a place of ego in the past, and that is okay. Let the damaging part of your past go. I will often tell myself, "That was a lesser version of myself who behaved that way. I didn't know better then." In this way, I give myself grace, use your memories for good instead of rumination. Find a comfortable balance where your ego works <u>with</u> you, not against you. Your healing comes from feeling the emotions from the past and changing them.

We become the best of self through service to others. How do we provide space for the ego while in service? Isn't service supposed to be selfless?

Many believe the ego is in direct contrast to the spirit. It is seen as a slight against God. I instead see that there's an important place for the ego when doing God's work. God is still present when you're in your ego. It all comes down to combining it with your spirit. It is the spirit that makes the realization, and it is the ego that actualizes it and answers the call. Essentially, the ego achieves God's work by enacting what the spirit is calling you to do. The intuition that comes through spirit is activated through the ego.

I need my ego to do God's work. It is where I manifest from. It provides my drive and my purpose. It keeps me in the present so I can teach about my experiences and be in service to others.

It is important to remember that true self-care and self-help are not achieved at any extreme. Success is found in the balance between two ends. It is found when we're not consumed with self and instead leave room for spirit. Once you are receptive to this, you can experience a higher level of calmness and confidence.

THE EGO ACHIEVES *God's* WORK BY ENACTING WHAT THE *spirit* IS CALLING YOU TO DO.

CHAPTER 8:
Journal Prompts

Reflect on society's perception of the ego: How has society shaped your understanding of the ego? Explore any beliefs or judgments you hold about the ego being a negative force that needs to be eradicated. How does this perception impact your personal growth and pursuit of success? Consider any conflicts or contradictions you may experience between societal beliefs and your own perspective on the ego.

Explore the role of the ego in personal growth and achievement: Reflect on specific instances where your ego has served as a driving force in your life. How has the ego pushed you to set goals, pursue success, and strive for more? How has it fueled your motivation and aspirations? Consider the positive aspects of the ego and how it can contribute to your personal growth and development. How can you harness the energy of the ego in a constructive way?

Embrace the power of dissatisfaction and desire: Reflect on the concept of dissatisfaction and its relationship with the ego. How has your innate desire for more propelled you forward and kept you on the creative plane? Explore instances where dissatisfaction has sparked innovation, growth, or pursuit of excellence in your life. How can you reframe dissatisfaction as a positive driving force rather than something to be avoided? Reflect on how to strike a balance between being content with what you have and maintaining a healthy desire for growth and improvement.

CHAPTER **NINE:**

Judgment-Free Zone

Nothing in the world is truly good or bad—it just <u>is</u>. It is our judgment and opinions that shape neutral events and define them as positive or negative.

Of course, it is totally natural for us to judge everything that exists in the world, including other people. We are always under scrutiny from ourselves and from others. It ensures our safety and helps us pick the social circles we want to exist within. This judgment also helps shape our larger community. As a society, we collectively play a part in defining the worth and meaning of something. The group creates a mindset that helps us settle on a shared opinion. Even if we don't agree with a judgment, it still exists as a consensus.

Oftentimes, we accept this consensus as the truth. However, once this consensus is dissected, it becomes clear what is fact and what was fabricated by society. It all comes down to distinguishing <u>truth</u> from <u>judgment</u>.

For example, think about what is labeled as junk food and what is considered nutritious. When it comes down to it, who is really saying that a bag of potato chips is bad for you and that an apple is healthy? Society is. At some point, people agreed with these labels for these particular foods and the labels stuck.

However, on its face, how bad is a bag of chips? Why does it have such a stigma attached? For the most part, the potato chips are innocent. Instead, it's the negative feelings surrounding eating the chips, namely the guilt and the shame, that create the negative seeds that are planted and breed bad gardens. It all comes down to that negativity weighing you down and making you less confident when going out in the world, even impacting the food you eat and the way you feel about it.

Instead of listening to the opinions of others and the labels attached to ideas, it is up to you to decide whether something is truly good or bad. Part of this process involves removing the negativity from certain situations and reframing them as positive. Once you alter your personal meanings and opinions, new possibilities will unfold before you.

Recently, I met a woman who shared what she considered a major problem: she couldn't gain weight. I know what you're probably thinking—*what an ideal problem to have!* Still, it was a source of frustration for her that I took seriously as I helped her sort it out.

When she mentioned this, I was reminded of an Abraham Hicks video. Essentially, Hicks states that it's not the food that you eat that determines whether or not the weight stays on your body - instead, it is your judgment that determines whether or not the weight stays on your body. In a sense, if you eat unhealthy food without the shame, guilt, and regret attached, you are less likely to gain weight. After noticing that this woman eats whatever she wants, including junk food, I asked her, "What do you think about the food that you eat?" She was thrown off by my question at first, so I explained further, "Do you think the food is wrong? That it's unhealthy? That you shouldn't have it?" Without batting an eye, she responded that she didn't consider this at all, explaining that she simply eats it because she likes it.

The simplicity of her response was shocking to me. Every single time I ate something that wasn't considered healthy, I felt bad about it. How could someone avoid this entirely?

It all comes back to your belief. If you believe in something being bad, it will likely exist in the world in that way. The only way out of this is to stop judging what you consider unhealthy behavior. Decide instead to indulge in junk food without beating yourself up. Enjoy what you want out of life, food included. This still involves moderation in what you eat, but it is equally important to change your perception so that you're not overly critical of yourself.

Let's consider another example: issues with alcoholism and staying sober.

When people say they are sober, they are implying that they have a drinking problem that they are solving. In this way, their life still revolves around alcohol; the idea of sobriety is tethered to the past and dragging them down in the present.

I recently met a man that was a recovering alcoholic. After congratulating him on his resolve, I asked how long it had been since he had a drink. He said, "Ten years." I replied, "I'm sorry, but what if you are not recovering from anything, but instead now exist in the new identity of a non-drinker?" In that moment, I saw that he was clinging to a past concept of himself; he was stuck in the judgment that at some point in his life before, he drank too much and can't handle his alcohol and has a certain weakness. That identity still lingers in his consciousness when it should be regulated to the past. His question should be this: Can I accept a new identity now that I don't drink? In this acceptance, he would find the effortless way.

ONCE YOU
ALTER YOUR
personal
MEANINGS AND
OPINIONS, NEW
possibilities
WILL UNFOLD
BEFORE YOU.

Of course, I've had my own share of struggles and can understand how hard it can be when they pop up in the present. At times in my life, I've been depressed. From there, I've been diagnosed by a doctor. I've been medicated for it. Still, I would not identify as a "person who was previously depressed" or a "recovering depressed person." It's not who I currently am. This is all in the past, along with other insecurities and issues that I had a hard time getting a handle of.

For years, I believed I was a problem that needed fixing. I had this belief that I was unhealthy, undisciplined, and lazy. This all made me want to enact drastic changes. I lost weight so I was no longer told that I was fat. I shrunk myself to fit into a certain mold that was more acceptable. I starved myself to meet the definition of skinny. This was all in the name of "health."

Based on societal pressures, I believed that health meant looking good. When I told others that I was going to get healthy, what I really meant was this: "I'm going to shrink my body down. I'm going to get skinny." The irony was that I wasn't actually doing anything that healthy. Depriving myself of food, going on a ketogenic diet devoid of carbohydrates, limiting myself to 800 calories a day, obsessing over my body shrinking, and hopping on the scale every single day to see if I'd lost any weight weren't practices that scream "health" to me. It all stemmed from my desire to look good when I thought I looked gross. It was never about prolonging my life or making my body actually feel good. I never looked at the food I was eating and thought, "This is going to give me vitamins and nutrients and fuel my body so that it functions properly." Instead, my thought process was, "I'm going to eat this apple simply because it's going to make me skinnier." There was a total lack of rationale. I imparted a delusion influenced by the diet industry, choosing vanity over the longevity of my vessel.

I soon saw that there are many people working within health care that are selling vanity under the guise of wellbeing. When selling weight loss products, supplements, fitness regimens, and programs, they are actually selling the idea that "skinny is better." With this, they equate being skinny with healthiness. The problem with pushing vanity as health is that, more often than not, when people use these diets or approaches to better health, they gain the weight back plus some. Furthermore, there is more and more evidence every day that does not correlate your appearance with health. There are people in thin bodies that are unhealthy; likewise, there are people in larger bodies that are in perfect health. Notice how you reacted to that statement and you will feel the judgments programmed into you.

The main problem is that the goal is weight loss, not a reframing of one's mindset. It's a short-term fix to a more nuanced problem. Regardless, I bought into it, trying my best to lose weight and satisfy a society that wanted me skinny. Unsurprisingly, I hated myself while simultaneously trying to become what I thought was the best of myself. I soon realized that this was what <u>everyone else</u> wanted me to be. It wasn't what I really wanted. Instead, what I wanted was for my body to last me a long time. I reframed my goals accordingly, asking, "How can I focus on my body <u>being taken care of</u> from this moment forward?"

With this decision, I had to release all the judgment of what I had done to my body in the years previous. The irony was that when I wasn't hyper-focused on looking better and instead approached health with an improved attitude, I did start to look better. I had a glow about myself, both from changing my body and changing my mindset.

The driving factor being "looking good" was no longer to get validation from others. Instead, the drive was to live a healthy long life. The main question became, "How can I take care of myself today?" instead of, "How can I lose a pound?" This simple shift in how I talked to myself and judged my behaviors made a world of difference.

How do we measure success—by the scale or by how we feel? The choice is yours.

How do we shift from a life overcome with judgment to a life full of positive self-expression?

While people imagine the better version of themselves that they strive toward, they often continue to be critical toward themselves in their daily lives. They actively disempower themselves while on the path toward empowerment.

When you notice yourself falling back into old habits, ask yourself: *When am I being critical? Where does this critique come from? How often does it bubble up?*

Once you pinpoint when it happens, it's easier to reframe the behavior. Every moment a critical thought pops up, you change it. If it helps, you can literally look at yourself in the mirror and say, "No, not today."

Separate from your own inner monologue, notice when other people are critical toward themselves. Consider when you show the same behavior.

Beyond that, think back on when other people have been critical toward you. Oftentimes, their critique, as well as your reaction to it, mirrors your inner self. To put it simply, a judgmental comment is often just your own judgment reflected back at you.

Recently, someone said something to me that was quite critical and caught me off guard. While they didn't intend for it to come across as judgmental, I got upset and called them out for being rude. It should have rolled off me; these types of comments usually do. Instead, what they said stuck with me. After some reflection, I realized I was triggered by what they said because there was something within me that believed it. I was simply getting back from them the energy I was putting off. In that moment, it was hard to hear. They reflected a criticism I had about myself, and coming from them it hit me harder. The beautiful thing was this was a great awareness for me to give myself more grace and more kindness and to criticize myself less.

Still, I was able to reframe it as a positive. My reaction hinted at a weakness within my subconscious mind and highlighted an area for growth. The next step was becoming a version of myself that sees no weakness. When I got upset, I reverted to a past version of myself that I don't aspire to be. Instead of sitting with this, I learned from it. It was evidence of places I could change for the better. Eternal forward motion isn't believing I'm perfect and have no room for improvement, but seeing that to be my best, I need to see the best in me right now. I always strive to be better, but self-hate is not the way towards that elevation.

Ultimately, I want to be a version of myself that doesn't get shaken by other people's judgments. I don't even want to notice the comments of others if they aren't constructive. I want to dismiss baseless critique as untrue and focus instead on moving forward and building a better reality. This doesn't mean we deny our blind spots. We should still seek out the opinions of mentors, leaders, and guides if we wish to elevate ourselves.

Still, this is easier said than done, especially when you are always being judged or looked down upon in the public eye. Every day, society echoes your imperfections back at you in the way it scrutinizes you, the way it makes you feel incomplete, the way it sells you a product that promises to move you closer to perfection. In the face of this, our subsequent shame and guilt and insecurity keep us trapped in the energy of wrongness. In response, we judge ourselves much too harshly and stay stuck in the stage of fixing ourselves so we can meet certain standards instead of simply being better.

Without releasing this shame and guilt we feel when we are judged, we will continue to perpetuate harmful realities. The best way forward is to turn your belief around and create an identity built from a loving perspective. This can only happen if you regulate your identity to respond to critique in a positive way, free from negativity. Until you can elevate up and out of these negative feelings, your identity isn't going to shift.

Oftentimes, an awakening or an epiphany prompts this elevation. For me, it came down to a simple decision to stop judging myself so harshly.

In 2019, I decided that I wasn't going to try to lose weight anymore. I was going to accept who I was. I wasn't going to stress about other people's judgment. I wasn't going to be stuck in my head worrying about how I looked. I was simply going to <u>be</u>.

When I decided to love myself where I was and believe that I was beautiful in my 300-pound body, I let go of the idea that I was a problem that needed fixing. I replaced insecurity and anxiety with a powerful self-identity. The concept of myself was now strong, powerful, and loving. This new model of growth and loving myself to become the best of myself was a powerful shift that changed my perception of my life greatly.

With this modification in my mindset, the self-hate was gone. When I decided to consider my health and happiness, I came about it from a loving, understanding perspective instead of self-loathing. It was a completely different energy that I was putting forward and it directly translated to a more fulfilling life.

The shift was simple: I now embodied a new version of myself that was accepting. Accepting is so important. Accept people for who they are; stop judging them. Accept situations for what they are; stop judging them. Accept the world for how it is; stop judging it. Accept yourself for who you really are.

Ask yourself:

Why do I judge others? What does it mean?
Why do I judge situations?
Why do I judge myself?
Why does feeling judged feel so damn uncomfortable?
Why would I move away from judgment, and why is a judgment-free zone
so important for my growth and becoming the best of myself?

Become the person that embodies empathy, acceptance, and appreciation. Move from judgment to gratitude and thankfulness. Exhibit this in your actions in order to feel it with others.

After all, who gave us the right to judge others? Who's in charge of judging us and telling us what's right or wrong? Nobody.

The feeling of inferiority does not come from God. It doesn't come from our highest self. It is a human creation. Furthermore, spirit does not judge. It doesn't test us. It only responds to you and the vibration that you're in. Judge less, love more.

CHAPTER 9:
Journal Prompts

Reflect on the power of consensus and personal truth: Explore the statement, "Oftentimes, we accept this consensus as the truth. However, once this consensus is dissected, it becomes clear what is fact and what was fabricated by society." How has societal consensus influenced your beliefs and judgments? Reflect on instances where you have questioned the consensus and discovered your own personal truth. How does discerning between fact and societal fabrication contribute to your sense of authenticity and personal growth?

Challenge the influence of external opinions: Reflect on the statement, "Instead of listening to the opinions of others and the labels attached to ideas, it is up to you to decide whether something is truly good or bad." How can you cultivate the ability to discern your own judgments and perspectives separate from external influences? Consider specific situations or beliefs where you are pressured to conform to societal opinions. How can you empower yourself to make independent judgments based on your own values and truth? Explore practices or techniques that can help you detach from external labels and opinions.

Embrace reframing and shifting perspectives: Reflect on the statement, "Part of this process involves removing the negativity from certain situations and instead reframing them as positive." Explore instances where you have successfully reframed negative situations or beliefs into more positive ones. How did this shift in perspective open new possibilities and expand your mindset? Reflect on the power of altering personal meanings and opinions. How can you actively practice reframing in your daily life to cultivate a more positive and empowering outlook?

CHAPTER **TEN:**

Inferiority

One of the biggest obstacles holding people back from ascension is the opinion that they're less than, especially in comparison to others. How can you ascend when you can never quite catch up?

This feeling of inferiority can often feel overpowering. It can become your way of being, a state you perpetually exist within that you're unable to shake. Oftentimes, you not only feel it; you verbalize it, telling yourself and others that you're not good enough, you're not smart enough, you're not beautiful enough. But for some, you don't express it outwardly but it's always there.

For me, it wasn't that obvious at first. I started to really become more aware of it when I started to study myself. The inferiority would show up in group settings more prominently. It actually started to show up when I started feeling it less. I remember in 2020, I got asked to speak on live events, trainings and summits quite often and was really well received. Eventually, I would go onto these speaking events with ease, no question as to what I would say or if people would resonate, no preparation or nervousness, no question if I would do a good job, just <u>knowing</u> I would. In these moments, I became aware that this was a different feeling than what I was used to. The old me would have prepped for hours the night before, would have been nervous, would have considered who might be on the training and maybe if they knew more than me and what that would be like, but not anymore.

I remember giving my first talk on Bob Proctor's virtual event with over 90,000 people signed up. The old me would have been so scared because how could I possibly measure up to the incredible Bob Proctor who had been teaching this for over 60 years! Would people know I was so new? Would people call me out for not knowing what I was talking about? Would people judge me? But what happened instead is that I became a version of myself who saw my worth, saw my voice as being unique and important. I remembered that we are all the same. Since no one is better than me, I am not less than anyone. I am not better, and no one is less than. These can be powerful mantras to remind you of how things really are when the feeling of being less than is prominent.

Like all emotions, the statement and being of "I feel inferior" has a vibration. Essentially, any time you feel inferior, there is a vibrational equivalent and a shift in your point of attraction. In the case of inferiority, it's a negative shift. When this energy translates to the outside world, it attracts other people who also feel inferior. When these two "inferior" people become intertwined, they need each other's constant affirmation to feel some semblance of confidence. This relationship quickly becomes codependent. I know this from experience. Two anxious attachment styles trying to provide for each other is a recipe for failure. Feeling insecure, less than, and unworthy all have a feeling. Sometimes it comes and goes but for most, it's part of the vibration you hold all the time. This heaviness, when released, will free you and you will find you attract from a completely different place.

If there was no one else in the world, we would rid ourselves of this inferior feeling, but this isn't realistic. The other is always present. However, what I can tell you is that it is possible to not feel less than. I made this shift myself, and I have seen countless others do it too. This is the energy you want to connect with.

In Dan Sullivan's *The Gap And The Gain*, he mentions the feeling of being in the gap—the space between where you'd like to go and where you currently are. Sullivan suggests that you want to instead be in the <u>gain</u>. When here, you are essentially becoming aware of all the ways in which you're doing better. You note what's working, the positive points of where you're at, and how all of this is moving you forward.

My approach is similar. It involves finding a healthy kind of confidence that includes collaboration with others instead of competition.

It can feel impossible to escape the cycle of comparison and the feeling of inferiority, especially in the modern world when everyone's lives are on display for public consumption. Our push to compare ourselves is often exacerbated by social media as we constantly watch what other people are doing with their lives. We become voyeurs, observing others and missing out on the life they are living, wishing we had the same. More than likely, this makes us feel less than. We might even bounce between being inspired in one moment and feeling less than the next.

On social media, we all want to craft a compelling story. We want to shape our lives into an interesting narrative. We want to share the highlight reels, only posting the best things that happen to us. With this in mind, many of us are averse to sharing the challenges and hardships.

As a result, everything is curated to look luxurious and perfect. People sell everything with a sparkly sheen. Just outside of the shot is real life. I think immediately to influencers showing their homes, moving all the clutter out of the shot so it looks perfect. Everything curated, luxurious, perfect. No sign of real life to be seen. When comparing yourself to something flawlessly framed that ignores all the imperfections, of course you're going to come up short.

I don't care about these comparisons. All I care about is if you are better than you were yesterday. I care if you are putting effort into incremental growth.

To combat the negative effects of social media, consciously make a decision to observe and become open to suggestions from people who <u>don't</u> make you feel less than. Seek out situations that make you feel inspired and empowered instead. Choose what you consume and what critique to take depending on the frame of mind that you're in. If you're in a bad mental space, going on social media will affect you negatively. In this instance, it's probably best to avoid observing others on social media and comparing their lives to the one you're living.

Focus on having an empowered state of mind and highlight the growth you've experienced. Like Sullivan said, you're in the <u>gain</u>. Then, when you see someone on social media crushing it, you think, "Look at them crushing it! I must be next."

It all comes down to the energy you are in when you consume social media or interact with others and the way you respond to that content. Become aware of your consciousness. Choose when you use social media and when you don't. Measure how you feel. Know what makes you feel good when you consume it and what makes you feel crappy. React accordingly and consume it in a way that is productive for you and your growth. Filter out what is harmful. Consider the time of day and how it impacts your emotions. For the most part, it's best to avoid hopping online first thing in the morning. When you do, you're allowing other people's lives to infiltrate you and set the tone for your day. Everything you see is suggestive to the subconscious mind. You want to start your day by suggesting an empowered idea to your subconscious.

Most importantly, remind yourself that <u>social media is not real life</u>. It's largely inauthentic. You're comparing yourself to someone's highlight reel. Of course, you can combat this and present something real. This can become one way to overcome comparison. So many influencers are showing their real lives, their real bodies.

Personally, I want to be authentic with everything I share, including my social media presence. After all, I sell transformation. If I were to say that everything was hunky-dory and I presented a staged perfection on my social media pages, I'd be selling a delusion. I'd be pushing an unrealistic idea that doesn't show the highs and lows of life. If I don't expose my ups and downs, I feel like I'm not treating my followers and clients with respect. Painting a picture that I have it all figured out isn't real, especially since I'm still over here expanding to become the best of myself as well. So I share my learnings through experience. I openly discuss my lung surgery in 2022 and subsequent growth that came from it, for example. If there is something I haven't shared, it's because it involves someone else and I'm respecting their privacy.

I'd rather show authentic parts of me. My ability to show vulnerable, difficult moments helps people connect and feel less alone as they start their journey toward change. I hope that the act of sharing my low points serves as a lifeline. I can only inspire trustworthiness if I am honest. This entire journey is about authenticity and integrity. Therefore, I live my truth. The way I am on social media is what you get in real life. This is why I've had quantum leaps, because I embody the material. It's not something I turn on and off. I exist within this space all the time.

To feel at one with yourself and avoid the trappings of the ego, it's up to you to achieve that same expression of authenticity. To do so, start with shedding the feeling of inferiority. You're not less than because you are learning and growing. You're not less than because you're having a hard moment. You're not less than because your life doesn't match the perfect lives everyone is living online.

How do I reframe a self-concept that involves an inferiority complex?

First, I notice whenever I feel inferior in my life, and I ask myself the following questions:

Where and when do I feel less than?
What is causing it?

Oftentimes, we feel inferior because we want to be the best and haven't yet achieved this "best" version of us in our mind. We see people all around us who appear to be creating success and it makes us feel less then, but the underlying inferiority still stems from within us. I also noticed in myself, an underlying feeling of inferiority that was present all the time. Everyone else knows more, does it better, has more experience, looks better, is more confident, etc. It took time but it was not hard to rid myself of it.

Since inferiority cannot exist in solitude, here are some guiding questions that may help you uncover where the feelings are activated:

Who do I think I am less than?
Who am I competing with?
Why do I think they're better?
What am I trying to measure up to?
What and how will make me measure up?

After you do some introspection, I would recommend becoming solution-oriented and moving from being in <u>competition</u> to being in <u>collaboration</u>.

Years ago when I first launched my own business, I excelled at the position and swiftly rose the ranks. It was not long before I reached the number two spot in the world on the leaderboard for this company. I remained there for months on end. Even though this status was inspiring to others and I had so much to be proud of, I still felt less than. I was always number two. There was always one person who eked out that top spot most times. Because of the perceived competition and me not winning it, I felt less than. Instead of recognizing how amazing I was doing and celebrating my success, I was stuck feeling unsatisfied with my status.

At a certain point, I recognized this comparison made me feel inferior. I made a change to my perspective. I decided to stop competing, and I mentally removed myself from the competitive mindset. I asked myself, "Why is being #1 important to me? What do I gain when I reach #1?" This reflection allowed me to see that winning meant I was worthy, it meant I would finally measure up. I think competition is something we create to inspire people, but often it has a negative effect. When competition is healthy, it moves the ego into action and gets you to push past some of your limits. But, it can become unhealthy when it has you question your own worth.

Once I realized the competition wasn't serving me, I removed myself from it. At first, I didn't announce I was leaving; I just stopped paying attention to the competition and just paid attention to bettering myself and my sales. This really helped. Nothing changed but what I focused upon. One thing I did on purpose was send the #1 salesperson tons of love and congratulations. This took me out of competition and the observance of someone doing good. I took myself back into being inspired.

We are prisoners of perception and perspective. It shapes our happiness and sense of self, even as we are achieving great levels of success. What we can do with this is use it to our advantage. This starts with a rejection of competition when it no longer serves us. Competition is all well and good when it's for fun and when it advances you past your limits, but it can be very limiting. Moving out of competition and into collaboration can move you to a high level of awareness.

This shift will allow space for more growth because you won't be held back by comparison and the threat of feeling inferior. Why do you want to win? Why do you want to outperform another? This was learned, and freeing when you move into collaboration.

I've observed this throughout my coaching career, as a peer to many other coaches. Even though a mentor's goal is to help people move forward in their lives, it can appear to be a very competitive place. The competition that arises often in this industry involves comparing how much money you've made to other coaches who share their successes of this nature in public and measuring yourself against this accordingly. If you choose to pay attention to this, and not fully be in your spirit, it can feel competitive instead of inspiring. Even though you are an incredible coach, your client's are winning, and you are making such a brave impact on this world, not making money like "them" can make you feel diminished in your own view of your success. This false sense of competition is not real. No one is competing. I think back to being a nurse. I can't imagine feeling like I'm competing with the nurse helping the client in the room next to me.

Like any career or livelihood, the problem comes from comparing your work to other people's success in the same field. The optimal response is to not see people in a competitive manner and to see them instead in a collaborative manner. No one is competing with you. Each of us is on our own growth journey. Our job, after all, is to help each other, not cause harm or enact conflict. This is much easier to achieve once you're aware that you are working alongside someone else.

One of my greatest professional and personal relationships is with someone who society would deem my "competition." We mastermind quarterly and empower each other to reach our goals alongside one another. While there are other coaches in this industry who see me in a competitive manner, I see them as a mentor, an influence, or an example to learn from.

As you shift from competition into collaboration, you give energy to your strengths and goodness while boosting your self-concept and the self-concept of others.

What, then, does collaboration entail?

In direct contrast to comparison, the collaborative plane is the creative plane. Here, one experiences existence, synchronicities, flow, ease, and connection with others. You are one of many helping others, combining to have a positive impact in the world. It's less about your ego and more about your calling, about your spirit.

Most of all, the collaborative plane understands the law of compensation. The more people you help and the more people you collaborate with in helping other people, the better you will do and the better you will be. It all works in synergy. Instead of competing over resources, we recognize the universe for the abundant place it is and become a vibrational match to more. You shining does not take away from anyone else, just as their shine doesn't take from yours.

To achieve this state of collaboration, it's important to become aware of and reject the beliefs and ways of being that society programmed into you that do not serve you. They once were the basis of your reality, but as I hope you have become aware of in this book so far, there is no set way of believing or living in this 3D world. We can see things differently and change our experience. Challenging common morals, beliefs, values, standards, and ideals has been my path to freedom. From there, you can develop new beliefs and morals that are more beneficial to yourself and others.

Each and every one of us is born into certain circumstances and belief systems that instill us with a sense of values and cultural norms. This is a paradigm that makes for a certain way of seeing the world and engaging with it. So these dominant feelings of inferiority, never measuring up, competition, and comparison were all learned. Your self-concept was then built around them. Based on these assumptions, you created an idea of what you can and cannot do, how important or valuable you are, and just how far in life you will be able to go. Those who are really engrained in these patterns aren't even aware of what they don't know, how life could be better, or even the potential that lies within.

Think about all the "rules" in your life that you didn't invent but are taken as true. Who decided that we are supposed to eat three meals a day? Who set the age of retirement? Who said we're supposed to get a college degree before entering the workforce? Do we really have to find our one true love and get married to feel whole? This is all a social construct that pressures what we're supposed to do. I often ask my students the question, "According to whom?"

For example, I had a private coaching client who had done amazing things in her business but never quite felt like she was doing enough. This feeling was deep in her subconscious and asking this question revealed some significant blocks related to her childhood. The originating belief is so important to uncover, and then ultimately replace. So, if we create a new belief "according to ourselves," then we become evidence of the proof of it all. I have beliefs that I am pretty sure I might be the only one I know who believes them but that doesn't bother me one bit, because I create my reality through my beliefs, and my reality is pretty damn amazing. It's always important to remember that what you believe to be true will always be your truth.

One belief that is engrained in most of us is that what other people think matters, and it matters a lot. We should absolutely care what the world thinks of us. And so we engage in this world in that way. Whenever we try on an outfit, we consider what people might think. When you're about to post a picture, you post from the perspective of how it will be received. You stop yourself from exploring a business venture because you imagine the critical response. We don't do things because we want to, but because it will look good, we "should" do them, or simply because everyone else is doing it. This can be stifling and lead to a lot of closed doors and missed opportunities. For so long, my life revolved around other people's opinions, and the most liberating thing was releasing them. It's not to say I never care what people think, because in business, feedback matters, but it doesn't influence the creation of my reality, the concept I hold of myself, or the actions I do or do not take in my life.

The most influential reframe I have ever made was to believe that my opinion of my own life matters the most. After all, who is the one who will actually live your life? You.

So how do we overcome feelings of inferiority? The one place to always turn to is your self-concept. What you believe about yourself will perpetuate, and you will express life through it. So, this place where inferiority exists in your consciousness, let's remove and replace it. The truth is, there is a version of you that exists already that knows their worth, steps into their power, sees their uniqueness as their magic, and blazes a trail that no one was brave enough to blaze up until now. Stop trying to be like everybody else.

The first step is to actually find out what YOU want out of life. What would be your perfect life? What human experience lights your soul on fire? What do you truly desire? There are infinite possibilities for yourself, and once you have an authentic answer to these questions, set your sights and move toward it with assuredness and confidence. Just because something hasn't been done before doesn't mean it's not possible. Dreamers change the world. The brave bring new visions into our life. The bold question old ways of doing things.

As you escape the feeling of inferiority, one thing to avoid is feeling superior. After all, rejecting inferiority is never about thinking that you're better than others. The truth is that no one is better than anyone else. So as we reject inferiority, we also want to steer clear of superiority. This is a great place to ensure your ego stays productive.

People could get caught up in this attitude as they find the right level of confidence. They may start to love themselves and start feeling superior. They might believe that if they have more money, they must be better at business. They might think that because they have more degrees, it must mean that they are smarter. They deduce that if they get a promotion, then they must be a better or harder worker. Even as they better themselves, they believe that because they are further along in their growth, they must be stronger. I used to believe this too, just from the inferior position. Now I see how either perspective isn't valuable.

The truth IS, THERE IS A version OF YOU THAT EXISTS already THAT KNOWS THEIR WORTH.

Why do we believe this? It's arbitrary. It's not a healthy perspective for anyone to have, even if they are in a position where they are sharing their guidance or expertise. I avoid this feeling entirely, especially in my interactions with clients. People hire me to be their coach because I can help them with their awareness. They don't hire me thinking that I'm better than them. I'm not. I just have wisdom, experience, and knowledge that they are not yet aware of. This doesn't make me better. The most important part of mentorship is that someone outside of you can help you see what you can't see in yourself because you are too close to yourself.

CHAPTER 10:
Journal Prompts

Reflect on the impact of feeling inferior: Explore the statement, "One of the biggest obstacles holding people back from ascension is the opinion that they're less than, especially in comparison to others." How has the feeling of inferiority affected your personal growth and sense of self-worth? Reflect on specific instances or patterns where this feeling has been overpowering. How does this feeling influence your point of attraction and overall vibrational state? Consider the emotional, mental, and energetic shifts that occur when you experience feelings of inferiority.

Embrace incremental growth and self-comparison: Reflect on the statement, "All I care about is if you are better than you were yesterday. I care if you are putting effort into incremental growth." How does this perspective shift the focus from comparing yourself to others to focusing on personal progress? Explore instances where you have experienced incremental growth and its positive impact on your self-esteem and overall well-being. How can you cultivate a continuous improvement mindset and celebrate your achievements, regardless of external comparisons?

Consciously curate your social media and surroundings: Seek out situations that make you feel inspired and empowered instead. How does your social media consumption and immediate environment impact your sense of self-worth and comparison to others? Reflect on the people, accounts, and situations that uplift and empower you versus those that trigger feelings of inferiority. How can you consciously curate your social media feed and surround yourself with individuals who inspire and support your growth? Consider practical strategies for creating a positive and empowering environment.

CHAPTER **ELEVEN:**

Being Limitless

One thing I hope you walk away with strongly in your consciousness after reading this book is that the best of yourself is limitless. You have always been, you just forgot, and I'm blessed to be the one to remind you.

Remember when we were kids and we would be asked what we wanted to be when we grew up? We chose things based on what we saw, what we believed possible, what we knew. But in reality, anything was possible. We could have chosen to be anything, literally anything.

This means shedding certain self-imposed constraints that keep you from progressing.

When I consider the best of myself, I always consider all three planes: spiritual, intellectual, and physical. This is a great place to consider where you are limited. Some of these limitations are external, an outside force that dictates your circumstances or situation. This can be something beyond your control that puts you in a position of inequality. It can also be something that you have the power to possibly change. This often shows up in language like, "I can't do this because so-and-so won't let me," or, "That is not possible because of my current situation." In these situations, we believe our outside world limits us, which may or not actually be true.

One example that instantly comes to mind is the glass ceiling for women. This refers to the concept that there is only a certain amount of money that women can make and that men are usually making more. News stories have come out that prove this to be true. So, many people hear that and see a road to travel that will be harder. They don't see the possibility of making more than a man and act in that assumption. Personally, I believe this is the type of limitation that you must remove yourself. Instead of trying to change the outside world, change how you see it. I would break through the glass ceiling with my own consciousness. This might end up being your experience, but it certainly is not my type of attitude. And guess what? It's not. I created my own company, became the female CEO, and made that glass ceiling obsolete.

Another form of limitation exists on the intellectual plane, meaning, they exist in your mind, they come from within. These include restrictive thoughts that tell you what's worth pursuing, how far you can push yourself, and what you believe holds you back. For the most part, these are learned behaviors that don't reflect reality.

Regardless of whether your limitations are external or internal, the first step is finding out how to break free from them.

Start by listing all the ways you've felt limited in your life. What external forces keep you constricted? Do they involve money? Time? Family? Physical ailments?

Next, focus on limits in your thinking. What ideas force you to exist within a box? Are these ideas coming from an outside influence or are you creating them? Which of these constrictions come across as arbitrary?

It's important to know what is constructed by humans and presented as truth when it really is ritual. When considering the intellectual or physical plane, there are so many imaginary walls that keep us in place and dissuade us from questioning what is possible. When ruled by man-made customs, laws, and opinions, we come to believe that every resource is limited, that our options are finite, that there are certain things we simply can't achieve. This all works together to keep us stationary.

Spirituality has become an incredible practice to expand my awareness of what's possible. The spiritual plane is abundant and infinite. It provides an unlimited supply of resources to meet your demand. This spiritual space is ideally where we want to be acting from.

Of course, this shift toward the spiritual plane can feel uncomfortable, especially if we've spent our lives believing these limits were unwavering. It's easy to reject what we consider to be impossible. Oftentimes, we fight for our limits because we believe they stem from our identity and can't be upended. We lean into all the reasons why we can't do something, even if this limitation doesn't serve us. Throughout this process, we fail to realize that the only thing limiting us is that belief.

There is this thing we learned: in order for it to be worthwhile, it has to be hard. Sometimes it's about letting it be easy—that is the real surrender. What if you aren't limited? What if you aren't blocked or stuck? What if you can easily decide?

Don't argue for your limitations or lean on excuses that restrict you. Instead, fight for your possibilities and your potential.

Our memory is a higher intellectual faculty that has many incredible functions for getting us through our lives faster and more efficiently, but it can be limiting if we don't use it to our benefit. We are limited by what we've already experienced. These experiences become the basis of our continued reality. Because this happened, I expect it to happen again. Because I didn't achieve this last time, I expect I won't achieve it again. When we exist so much in our memory, we are not existing in our imagination, so we believe whatever the past tells us. The past only predicts the future if you believe it to and if you allow it to. This belief builds walls around us that close off certain possibilities. These walls grow stronger and higher as one becomes more steadfast and solidified in their beliefs. In this way, we only go as far as our minds will go.

One thing that has helped me in my journey is to only use my memory for good. There are experiences, challenges, and past events that exist in one place only, your memory. If you forgot about it, it's quite literally like it never happened, right? This is where at times I will quite literally pretend something never happened, or that it does not exist. What I am doing here is very intentionally focusing what my mind is focused upon. Remember everything just is, it's not good or bad, it just exists, and so forgetting it ever happened removes the emotional attachment to it.

Forgetting or pretending something didn't happen will work for things like last month's decrease in your sales, that slipup you made speaking on stage during your last event, and falling in NYC in the rain in front of a lot of people and being mortified (this one really happened to me).

I will caution you to use this tool when appropriate and not to suppress emotion. So, when something meaningful to you has occurred and you are emotionally attached to it (you feel some kind of way), we do not want to just pretend it didn't happen or suppress the experience but allow yourself to feel and heal (a later chapter will discuss my perspective on this).

Despite the tendency to place limits on yourself, there's still hope. A shift can happen in an instant. If your mind can impose these limits, it also has the power to remove them. It means making a decision to see what's possible instead of what is.

I love to think of a jar with a lid. There's only so much that can fit in the jar with the lid on, but remove the lid and you can absolutely overflow with anything you have ever wanted and in whatever quantity. With a lid in place, a jar is only able to hold so much. This lid represents your limitations, some invented and others imposed. What I can tell you is that none of these limits are real. They only become your reality when you believe in them yourself. Your task is to remove this lid.

As you then move into being limitless, allow yourself to be open to possibility and see things that most people don't allow themselves to see. Believe in ideas that might not make sense.

Step into uncharted territory, trusting it will take you somewhere unexpected.

As you expand your consciousness and create more space and potential, everything you can see or imagine can become reality. Once it is seen, what was before impossible becomes available. My greatest strength has been in taking something that was once impossible and making it possible (in my mind), then bringing it into the physical with faith.

The biggest hurdle during this transformation is overcoming imposed limitations.

As children, we are born into limitations. We always had rules forced on us and were told that it was fact. This shaped our worldview and made it much more difficult to peer outside the box. The process of growth and maturity involves removing these limitations that were imposed on us from an early age.

Everyone still lives within these limits to some extent. It is part of being human and existing within a community. I fall victim to my limits from time to time. Luckily, I've usually been able to rationalize them and move beyond them. This helps when coaching others to rise above their limits and escape the urge to stay small and inhibited.

We shouldn't believe that certain things aren't possible. On the contrary, nothing is impossible. Michael Singer presents specific examples of what we used to deem impossible in his book *Living Untethered*, imploring you to be in awe of where you live, what you've experienced, and what we've done as a species.

Much like Singer, I'm in awe of what we as humans have been able to achieve. You can't tell me something that we cannot do without it being disproven. For example, the idea of flying an airplane hundreds of years ago felt miraculous, but now it is commonplace. Now, we have the ability to video chat with anyone in the world; you can only imagine how people a century ago would see this. They'd probably call it magic.

This universe is absolutely limitless. Along with this truth comes immeasurable gratitude, happiness, and abundance. It is up to us to expand our capacity to experience it.

Why do we think we can't do something, have something, or be something? In a world full of astounding advancements and inventions, why do we still cling to a limited mindset?

Oftentimes, we give this abundance of possibility to the other, all while rationalizing why we're not involved: "Let's leave this to the scientists or the tech industry. This is better suited for a PhD student. I'm not smart enough to achieve that. I don't have the time or the know-how to explore that." We believe that others have something that we simply lack; they know something that we could never know.

This belief flows from a place of insecurity and inferiority. It keeps us from attaining something bigger and better than what we're experiencing now. It restricts us from being creative and productive. These limits only exist in your mind. It's simply a state of being that you have to replace.

Take on the millionaire mindset to tap into limitlessness. Truly believe that you can be anything and do anything. This is where you find the best of yourself. There's no end to how much better you can get over the course of your life. There is always a higher level of every single emotion. It comes down to opening up your capacity to tap into and experience those higher levels.

Persist toward this path regardless of outside influence. Whether others say you can or you can't, you do it anyway. You have the choice to accept the limits or reject them; that is the control and power that you hold within yourself.

BE
realistic
AND EXPECT
miracles.

Be realistic and expect miracles. Don't believe that miracles are just magic or divine intervention. Instead, I see them as commonplace. They occur all the time once you shift your mindset to accept that the world is limitless.

I've battled self-made limits throughout my life. The limits of my body led me to believe I was flawed. I believed that I wouldn't achieve success until I was in a thin body. I thought that I wouldn't make money or have a profitable business until I lost some weight. While blowing out my birthday candles for 37 years, I wished to be skinny. It became an overwhelming obsession. If I would have let go of this and loved myself years ago, I likely would have lived a very different life—one that was more fulfilling, much like the life I lead right now.

How I thought about myself created the flaw and the limit. It took removing the belief that being overweight was bad to shed the limits it created. With this belief gone, my business and self-esteem skyrocketed.

Continual growth and expansion are the cornerstone of becoming the best of yourself, and this is the goal I am focused upon every single day. As I grow through experience, it is valuable to share with you some of my greatest limits and how I overcame them. I share with you in hopes that you will see in you a similar possibility for growth and be influenced to overcome instead of fall by your limitation.

In 2022, I was on Cloud 9. My business was booming. Despite the good news, I suddenly got sick. I fell ill with pneumonia that trapped my right lung and nearly killed me. After a year where I had peaked in my career and personal life and celebrated numerous successes, 2022 was not turning out how I had hoped.

During my recovery, I questioned why this all happened. If I was doing well, shouldn't I feel healthy? Why would sickness hit me at one of the highest moments of my life?

I soon realized that becoming sick was a protection mechanism. I had reached the upper limits of myself. I was reinventing myself and was close to becoming my best. On a subconscious level, this frightened me. My response was self-sabotage.

This sickness caused a shift. I gained awareness about the ways in which we disrupt our progress just as we are about to enact substantial change. As we grow accustomed to our limits and shortcomings, we are subconsciously committed to ideas that act as restraints. It's like driving through life with your parking brake on.

When we break free, it feels unfamiliar. One response is to fall back into those shortcomings because they feel comfortable. At your core, you are unconsciously <u>committed</u> to a limitation that doesn't serve you.

You end up asking yourself: *Am I supposed to stay where I was? Am I supposed to believe what I was told? Am I supposed to be left longing for more?* An escape from your limits could translate as survivor's guilt, especially if you escaped rags to enjoy riches. You might feel you're leaving others behind. Just remember that this movement upward helps everyone, not just yourself. After all, you don't cure poverty by staying poor. It involves change and a reframing of your limitations, not a commitment to the idea that you will forever be impoverished.

I know now that I was unconsciously committed to the idea of carrying extra weight. I kept returning to this idea, perpetuating it because I felt it was part of my identity. Even though consciously I asked for thinness, every time I lost weight, I would fall off the wagon. Something would happen in my life that would throw things out of whack—a loss, a fight, even something positive like a party. Whatever the influence, I was suddenly off the deep end and self-sabotaging. With every weight loss quest, I was getting closer to my upper limit. The response from my subconscious was rejection: "Nope – you're getting close to a new identity, a new level in your growth and that's uncomfortable, so let's go back to safety. Let's return to what we know: gaining and maintaining weight."

After more intentional self-awareness, I started to really see the times in my life that I neared my upper limit. Whenever I achieved a certain milestone and was reaching even higher, I would drop back down. I wasn't allowing myself to rise to the next level of consciousness. Now that I notice it, I take note of what triggered it, and I actively dismiss whatever influence drags me down. This upper limit showed up for me in illness, in sabotaging behaviors, and the fear of rejection. So, going forward, instead of giving in to indulgence, to fear of illness, or to rejection, I empower myself to stay the course and focus more on the desired outcome. With understanding comes greater awareness and managing of my upper limiting behaviors. Notice when you are going back and redirect yourself.

Further into my journey, something quite interesting was revealed. The shame and guilt associated with carrying extra weight was "heavy" in itself, but I also found an underlying assumption that, because I was overweight, I was unhealthy and that I was lazy. Was this true? What we believe to be true is how we express life; it's the law of expression. So, as long as I saw myself as unhealthy, I made unhealthy choices. So, I decided to BE healthy. How would I feel as a healthy person, what thoughts would I have about myself, and what ways would I behave? As long as you see extra weight in the mirror and judge it, the longer it stays (which is not a bad thing if you love your curves like I do). The longer you believe you are unhealthy, the longer you behave in a way that matches that. So, as I've said before, I'm loving myself to become the best of myself, health included.

One important reminder: never judge yourself whether you have bypassed a limit or not. Giving yourself grace is what separates those who love themselves and those who do not. You will never be perfect and you will always be (part) human.

I'M LOVING *myself* TO BECOME THE *best* OF MYSELF

CHAPTER 11:
Journal Prompts

Explore self-imposed constraints and limitations: Reflect on the statement, "Becoming your best involves creating a limitless version of yourself. This means shedding certain self-imposed constraints that keep you from progressing." What internal limitations or restrictive thoughts have you identified within yourself? How do these thoughts impact your beliefs about what is worth pursuing and how far you can push yourself? Reflect on the origins of these limitations and consider whether they truly reflect reality or are inventions of your imagination.

Challenge restrictive thoughts and beliefs: Reflect on the statement, "These include restrictive thoughts that tell you what's worth pursuing, how far you can push yourself, and what you believe holds you back." Identify specific thoughts or beliefs that you feel may be holding you back from reaching your full potential. How do these thoughts limit your perception of what is possible for you? Reflect on experiences or moments when you have challenged and overcome such limitations. How can you cultivate a mindset that challenges and replaces these restrictive thoughts with more empowering beliefs?

Embrace the limitless possibilities: Reflect on the statement, "For the most part, these are inventions born from your imagination that don't reflect reality." How can you shift your perspective to embrace the idea of limitless possibilities? Explore moments in your life when you have transcended self-imposed limitations and achieved something beyond what you initially believed was possible. Reflect on the potential within you to create a version of yourself free from these constraints. How can you cultivate a mindset of expansiveness and embrace the reality of your limitless potential?

CHAPTER **TWELVE:**

When I started studying with Bob Proctor, he said something that struck me as profound:

"You are not your body. You are <u>in</u> your body."

Essentially, what he meant was that the body you are in is simply your vessel. You are much more than a physical thing. This was enlightening. What I have since learned is that my body doesn't define me unless I believe it does. Just as you are not your body, your body is also not your identity and you are not what you look like.

For my entire life, I believed I <u>was</u> my body, Kathleen was the meat suit that I was in, and there wasn't anything else to it. I believed that to my core. When I looked in the mirror, I believed I was my body and nothing more beyond that.

It took me a while to realize that I was instead a "being" that is <u>aware</u> of myself. I am a "being" that is <u>aware</u> of my body. What kind of being was I? A spiritual being. I see now that I am one with spirit flowing through my body. This allowed me to release a lot of the pressure that I had placed on my physical form as well as the judgment of others.

When earning my psychology degree, I learned about a concept called "the invisible audience," and I haven't forgotten about it since that day more than 20 years ago. My professor explained that the ego thinks that there's an audience watching it at all times. If we believe we are being watched, we naturally behave differently. Essentially, many people walk around like there is this invisible audience, like they are on show all the time, when in reality, everyone is too busy with their own life and ego.

This idea really resonated with me because I've always been quite self-conscious. I had an acute awareness of how I looked at all times—this worry was amplified everywhere I went. I felt I was being scrutinized by others around me all the time. This made me shy and reserved. The source of the problem was that I had an overinflated sense of self that caused great discomfort. Because I felt I was flawed, it was like my flaw was on show for the invisible audience all the time. This was not my spirit, but my ego, making it about me when it never was. No one was walking around looking at other people's stomachs. They were concerned with themselves and their own perceived flaws.

When the professor explained the term, he paired it with an exercise. In front of a lecture hall full of 300 people, he said that he did something for the class and wondered who was paying attention. He asked if anyone noticed a man in the bright orange shirt that came into class late and dropped his books before he took his seat. Out of 300, only three people raised their hands. After this answer, he played back a video showing exactly what happened. This man entered, had a full-blown kerfuffle, then sat down. Barely anyone noticed even when we were shown something quite disruptive. We are all too consumed by chatting to the person next to us or preparing for class. We were not an audience for this one man. It was a beautiful way of putting my social anxiety into perspective. I realized that if we believe we are being watched, we move about the world differently, and many of us believe this is the case.

What we believe about our vessel shapes our reality. The belief that we are beautiful translates to us moving with beauty and grace. On the other hand, if you believe you are ugly, this will shape how you express yourself as well but in the opposite. I can feel my old insecurities pop up as I write this. I remember when I used to be getting ready for events and I would be so consumed with finding an outfit that was slimming, that hid my body rolls. I was so worried people were going to judge me that I was all consumed, and if i'm being honest, I didn't show up to many events because of this fear.

I have a very successful member of my coaching community who has been a helpful mirror for my previous insecurities. She was a former model; unsurprisingly, she is stunningly beautiful. Still, this became what she now perceives as a limitation. Because she saw herself as beautiful, she believed she would be successful. She saw it as a major advantage. Once she was done modeling, she wondered, "What do I do now? Without the focus on beauty, what do I have to offer that will translate to success?"

She had to understand that it wasn't the beauty that made her successful, but the belief that she holds about herself that did. This is the same for everyone. Believing you are successful, no matter the circumstance, breeds limitless success. Remember the emotional conception of yourself—this is what I am talking about here. How you feel about your body is a vibration, and you are walking around with it every single day.

Still, it's difficult to avoid caring about how you look, especially when looks play a significant societal role. To a degree, it is important, but not in the way you'd imagine.

HOW YOU FEEL
ABOUT YOUR BODY
IS A *vibration*,
AND YOU ARE
WALKING
AROUND WITH IT
every
SINGLE DAY.

Ultimately, it's about dressing in a way that makes <u>you</u> feel empowered and confident, and it's less about dressing for others. It's important to feel good about yourself and to feel comfortable in your own skin. Shift into what you believe is sexy or beautiful. Changing your style can assist in changing your beliefs. For example, I used to believe that dressing sexy was showing skin. Now I believe it is sexier to be covered but to wear a form-fitting outfit. I also believe it is sexy to dress powerfully, for example, wearing all black or a great belt. Both inspire specific feelings and instill me with different kinds of confidence, which shifts my thinking and the way I carry myself in the world.

Your confidence creates your sex appeal, regardless of size or shape. People respond to this confidence, not necessarily your body. They are reacting to what you believe about yourself. It may be helpful to create relative truths about your body and decide what you believe. Now that I love myself, I get a completely different reaction from people. While we are taught what other people think matters, the world has failed to teach us that what we think about ourselves influences what people think of us. So which comes first? Love yourself, forget about what people think, and just be your bad self.

Where does our physical appearance and longevity of our vessel come into play when becoming the best of ourselves? Which voices should we listen to? Who says we should look this way, behave this way, or be like this or that?

What I have learned is that what we believe to be true will forever be our truth, so why not believe something empowering about ourselves? It all comes back to taking our limitations and turning them into superpowers. It's about shaking up traditional thinking and instead taking on your truth that isn't imposed by those around you.

People are used to a plus-sized woman being self-conscious, shy, and maybe even being "the funny one." This has become socially accepted. It's also accepted to be fat shamed and made to feel less than because of your size. But this doesn't have to be your truth. Only if you choose it to be. The question becomes: *How do I break free from this stigma or societal belief?*

When I walked into Bob Proctor's Studio in Ontario, Canada, and met him in person to receive my silver and gold pins, I noticed a thought he had about me. He looked at me, and I could feel that a thought or opinion had popped in his head. While I didn't know what it was, I chose to ignore it and just be my authentic and confident self. Part of me worried it was judgment. Was he shocked that a plus-size woman had just done something so incredible? But instead, I let that thought go and chose not to give it any more focused attention. The ceremony was beautiful, I felt celebrated, and my friendship with Bob grew.

It wasn't until 6 months or more later, when he wrote the forward for my first book *Becoming the One* that he finally revealed what he thought. I received a phone call from Bob, and he told me he wanted to tell me something personally that he did not mention in the foreword. He said he had a thought about me when I first walked into his studio that day. He told me, "The day you came to the studio was the first time in my 87 years that I had come into contact with a woman of a larger stature that did not carry the vibration of guilt and shame about the way she looked."

I was floored. I did have those emotions of guilt and shame before, for most of my life, before I'd started studying with Bob. I carried it with me every single day. Bob's words were evidence that I had released these negative emotions. He felt it, and he <u>knew</u> it. I used to want to change myself so that feeling would go away, and finally, it was gone. The funny thing was that it felt effortless. I didn't quite notice it until someone observant pointed it out. The guilt and shame were gone because I changed the story about how I saw me.

When I left that day, I was left wondering:

What is it that you think makes you flawed regarding your appearance?
What is it about the way you look that impacts you?
How can you change the way you see your perceived flaw?
How can you make it more about who you really are instead of what you look like?

When we become the best of ourselves, we understand that who we are matters more than what we look like. It's that simple. Think about the people you're drawn to in your daily life. When you meet someone, you're likely more attracted to their overall energy than their appearance. It's about that connection that's deeper than the superficial or the physical. Furthermore, someone becomes more or less attractive to us the more we get to know them. Ultimately, if there's no connection or compatible energy, there's no attraction, regardless of beauty. They can be the best-looking person you've ever met and still fall short because of other features that are off-putting.

We determine what we find beautiful. This isn't dictated by society's standards. The best thing we can do is believe in the standards that we set ourselves.

It's hard to avoid the influence of beauty standards. How do you avoid these trappings and not buy into standards where you don't quite measure up?

For me, it was deciding to see beauty from a different angle. I began believing in the kind of beauty that fit my perspective and personal mind. With this shift, I put less value and worth in what I look like. From here, I sought out evidence that built on my belief. I discovered phenomenal plus-sized women that were achieving so much success. It made me feel more confident and comfortable in my own skin. It also made it clear that I was believing in the wrong ideals before.

For some people, their discomfort becomes so bad they seek out cosmetic surgery. They can't accept things about their body that they cannot change. This is a slippery slope. You fix one thing, and then the rest of your body isn't good enough in comparison.

Know that cosmetic surgery does not change who you are. There is no shift in your inner world or your actual worth. It doesn't change the way you see yourself or your attitude toward life. You're not a different or better version of yourself. If anything, the surgery amplifies your discomfort with your imperfections.

When we stop focusing on how we look, and focus on who we are, we truly start to see just how amazing we really are. Remember that you are not your body. You are so much more.

CHAPTER 12:
Journal Prompts

Reflect on the essence beyond your physical form: Explore the statement, "You are not your body. You are in your body." What does this mean to you? Reflect on moments when you have felt a deeper connection to your inner essence beyond the physical aspects of your being. How does this perspective shift your understanding of self-identity? Consider practices or experiences that help you cultivate a sense of connection to your inner self and detach from the identification solely with your physical body.

Embrace the power of self-perception: Reflect on the statement, "Believing what we do with our physical form shapes our reality. The belief that we are beautiful translates to us moving with beauty and grace." How does your perception of yourself and your body influence your overall experience of reality? Reflect on instances where you have experienced the impact of positive self-perception and how it has influenced your confidence, demeanor, and interactions with others. How can you nurture a belief in your own beauty and embrace the notion of moving through life with grace and elegance?

Explore the multifaceted aspects of your identity: Reflect on the statement, "Your body doesn't define you - it is simply something that you exist within. It's just a vessel. It is not your identity." How can you expand your understanding of self beyond physical attributes? Reflect on the various dimensions of your identity, such as your values, beliefs, passions, and relationships. How do these aspects shape your true essence and contribute to your sense of self?

CHAPTER **THRITEEN:**

Abundant Self

For me, the word *abundance* implies overflow. It means there's more than enough. This is paired with a desire for more and your receptiveness to receiving more. This abundance could come in the form of money. It could also arrive as love. It could show up as a promising new work opportunity. Abundance then has a feeling - one you can become yourself and then attract from. And the really exciting part? This expands infinitely. There is no cap.

What does it mean to be your abundant self?

Essentially, there are magnitudes of versions of yourself. There are a whole slew of ways that you can exist as you shape your identity, beliefs, and judgments. With this definition of self, there are multiple levels of abundance available for you to tap into. It all comes down to seeking out abundance instead of limitation. This requires existing within the creative plane and thinking solely from this space. It involves focusing on the art of expansion instead of staying stagnant. All the while, you remain optimistic.

As you discover this abundance, allow yourself to relate to success and the idea of one's best. One approach is to explore specific environments that make you feel successful. I like to stay in multi-million dollar homes or attend viewings with realtors in Malibu or look at properties in Hawaii. As I do this, I surround myself with possibilities of wealth that feel plentiful. It then becomes easier to imagine a similar future for myself.

Find what this looks like for you. Surround yourself with what feels good. What situation feels abundant or has a richness or positivity you'd like to pursue? This could mean getting the nicer coffee at the fancier shop. This could involve a ride on a fancy tour boat or a new home that's more exquisite. This could mean shopping somewhere more expensive, or at the very least window shopping at a store that's a bit ritzier. My clients know me well because I will drink water in a wine glass to tap into a fancier or more luxurious experience for myself.

It's easier to imagine yourself in these situations or spaces once they feel tangible and tactile. They become that much more prominent in your mind's eye. It's all about being able to relate to it, and if you can't relate, then it will never be available for you. The natural way in which abundance feels for you will give you clues to how receptive and open you are to receive it.

What, then, is the catch to seeing the universe as abundant and rich with resources? After all, isn't it true that things that go down must come up at some point? How does the ebb and flow of life factor into abundance? There's a cycle for everything. There exist clear ups and downs that create the rhythm of life.

Still, this doesn't imply that you'll become rich and then lose it all in a rhythmic fashion. Instead, being rich is a frequency of a vibration that you tap into. Once you begin vibrating at this frequency, you have to remain there without giving into your older self. If you're instead stuck in a pattern of making 5k a month, this will remain the same until we change the frequency of the vibration we're operating on. It means creating habits to build abundance instead of imagining your possible downfall when you're on an upswing.

ALLOW *yourself* TO BE *surprised* BY HOW MUCH GOOD CAN *exist* WITH AND *for us*.

Does this mean you're always going to make the same amount of money every month? It's not likely; there will still be some fluctuation. Regardless of this, you'll be positioned on the upper echelon, having good and bad months instead of trying to scrape by on working-class wages.

How can I feel abundant when I don't have any money? This is the most asked question I get related to wealth. My answer is this: You don't need money to feel abundant. Remember how I said abundance is a feeling? Well you can tap into this feeling right now. You can instead visualize it and in your imagination relate to it, experience it, and enjoy it. You can also pay attention to all the abundance all around you at any given moment, whether it's nature's abundance, the abundance of people, or the abundance of money available. The problem is, you don't think it's available to you, which keeps you from it.

Wealth, money, fame, and power are not quite the same. They aren't directly related, and they don't define being the best. If that were the case, being the best of yourself would be a shallow, empty pursuit that would be far from fulfilling. It is instead about freedom and finding a richness in new emotions, healthier relationships, and a positive self-concept.

This begins with accepting that there are no limits. Allow yourself to be surprised by how much good can exist with and for us. Open yourself up to infinite possibility and the law of universal supply.

The law of universal supply says that as long as there is a demand, the supply shall be given. And this supply is infinite, never ending, always fulfilled. It's a belief, and I have found it to be a very powerful belief to have. How do we know it's infinite? Because there are many people with an unlimited amount of money. It is not a resource issue but a receptivity issue, a mindset issue, and a vibration matching issue. So what does "demand" mean? This is the key to it all when it comes to abundance. When you ask for more, more is given. This does not mean asking for more but feeling less than. This does not mean asking for more money but feeling broke. The demand comes from your consciousness. Shift into a vibration of more, of plenty, of abundance, and you are then asking and being. Feeling abundant and asking for more money. Being grateful for what you have while asking for more.

The problem is that people are not demanding. Start acting in the assumption you are a millionaire and this creates the demand. Start planning for where the money will go, dream about the feeling of the million. This is exactly what I did and it worked. Over and over again.

Any belief that says true spirituality or enlightenment has nothing to do with money, or even rejects having more money, in my opinion is cutting itself off from our very source. To be truly connected to the divine is to see that we are meant to be prosperous and abundant, not to suffer in poverty. We are meant to have more and to show others how to have more as well. Not everyone wants to subscribe to these beliefs. And often it stems from past money wounds, so having compassion is key.

But having said that, becoming the best of yourself can be a lonely journey if you choose it to be. Throughout the process, it's easy to leave others behind as you evolve beyond your previous self. Just remember that you don't need someone else to feel fulfilled. There's no gap you need to fill to achieve your best. There's nothing that needs a replacement. It all stems from yourself. Feeling alone might simply mean you are going first, that you are blazing a trail, that you are bold and brave, and that YOU are making a difference.

One of the greatest things I've learned is that I don't need anybody to feel fulfilled. It is within me, and it has always been.

CHAPTER 13:
Journal Prompts

Reflect on the interplay between personal growth and relationships: Explore the statement, "Becoming the best of yourself can be a lonely journey if you choose it to be. Leaving others behind is easy as you evolve beyond your previous self throughout the process." How do you perceive the relationship between personal growth and the connections you have with others? Reflect on moments when you have felt a sense of isolation or distance from others during your personal growth journey. How can you strike a balance between self-evolution and maintaining meaningful relationships? Consider the ways in which personal growth can positively impact your connections with others.

Cultivate self-fulfillment without external dependencies: Reflect on the statement, "Just remember that you don't need someone else to feel fulfilled. There's no gap you need to fill to achieve your best. There's nothing that needs a replacement. It all stems from yourself." What does self-fulfillment mean to you? Reflect on moments when you have relied on external factors or relationships to feel fulfilled. How can you shift your perspective to recognize that true fulfillment comes from within? Explore practices and activities that cultivate self-fulfillment independent of external dependencies.

Embrace your personal journey while honoring connections: Reflect on the balance between personal growth and maintaining connections with others. How can you continue evolving and becoming the best version of yourself while also nurturing and supporting the growth of those around you? Reflect on the importance of self-care and self-focus while remaining mindful of your personal growth's impact on your relationships. How can you communicate and express your evolving self to others in a way that fosters understanding and mutual support? Consider strategies for integrating personal growth with the dynamics of your social connections.

CHAPTER **FOURTEEN:**

Taking Things Personally

Growing up, my family used to tell me that I was always taking things *so* personally. Other people would repeat a similar sentiment before telling me that what they had said was being misconstrued. "That's not what I meant; *that's how you took it.*" I would get so upset and feel like they were disrespecting me. No matter what anyone said, I believed it was a "them" issue. But now, I believe otherwise. I was taking everything personally and I was hurting my own feelings. I remember the lightbulb moment when I heard the idea that no one can hurt your feelings but yourself.

Our feelings get hurt because we choose to perceive whatever was said in a certain way with a meaning that hurts our feelings, ego, and sense of self. During that time, I was a version of myself that relied on other people's validation to make me feel good and whole. When I wasn't in a state of receiving external validation or recognition, I wasn't whole. So, when I picked up what felt like criticism from the people around me, I effortlessly took on the burden of criticism and let my inner insecurities bruise my feelings.

This neurotic behavior harms us and puts us into unnecessary suffering and disappointment that affects how we see ourselves, our relationships with others, our business, and our potentiality. So how can we solve this unnecessary pain? By understanding and accepting that other people's behaviors and actions and the world's impact around us *are not about us, but a reflection of us.*

This quote from Bobbi Chegwyn hit me in all the feels:

> *"Your perception of me is a reflection of you; my reaction to you is an awareness of me."*

I firmly believe that the root of many obstacles you'll encounter in life exist to keep you from being the best of yourself. There will be times when people leave our lives, our businesses, or our relationships, and we'll be impacted. There will be wars, market crashes, pandemics. In the wake of all this, we'll be forced to make important decisions that cannot rely on our egos or feelings alone. How can we ensure that we are right in spirit to make these tough calls? How can we make sure we're centered enough with ourselves to not get thrown off course when these things happen? Our biggest challenge is to look these ego-shaking events and experiences in the eye and reframe them as opportunities where we can ask: *Is this really about me? How can I be compassionate if it isn't? How is this a reflection of me?*

Taking things personally leads us to disappointment and strains our relationships with others. Sometimes, we misconstrue a difference in beliefs or paradigms as a slight against us and who we are, when truly it has nothing to do with us or our relationship to another person.

For example, I'm an "on-time or be early" kind of person. This means that when I say our meeting is at 2:00, I will be there at 2:00 or before. I've met and encountered people whose paradigm allows for being late, meaning these people will show up to our 2:00 meeting at 2:15 or even later.

In a past version of myself, if someone didn't show up on time, I would take that action as disrespectful and get very offended. In my brain, the story I was telling myself was: "This person is disrespecting me and disrespecting my time. They are making me wait. How dare they?"

Obviously, you can see how loud my ego and insecurities were when these events happened. But in reality, the other person's tardiness was never about me! It's a difference in beliefs, where two different paradigms are meeting. This person isn't intentionally saying, "I'm going to disrespect your time so I'm going to be late." It's more so about this person not believing that they are an on-time person. They are a chronically late person with a late paradigm. Their belief isn't that being late is a bad thing, that it is acceptable to be 15 minutes late, and they might not even be aware that it impacts another person negatively. Who says which is right and which is wrong? If two people who are chronically late go out on a date, neither will even notice they aren't on time! Moving out of judgment is a beautiful way to release the angst when different paradigms meet. And neither is wrong, only if and when that belief system becomes limiting or when a new one can become freeing for that person.

Now, the person who is perpetually late can ask themselves: *How can I aim to be more on time so that people feel more valued and understood? What is it about me that continues to want to be late all the time?*

The always on-time person can ask: *Is this person running late about me? Can I be a bit more flexible in my timing? Or perhaps I can plan for a later arrival knowing this person will be late.* It's all about greater understanding. By not taking on someone else's belief system as a personal attack against you, you free yourself. The "always late/always on time" paradigm is part of one's consciousness, and it can change by choosing a new belief system.

Sometimes it's not so much the paradigm of another person that stresses us out. Instead, it's their actions towards us that we perceive as being about us. Not only do we unnecessarily put ourselves through suffering by taking in someone's behavior as being about us, but we'll often create a narrative around this that perpetuates our hurt feelings into a bigger gap of misunderstanding and pain.

Let's say you have a friend that stops calling you out of the blue. If you're working from a place of insecurity and ego, your brain will tell you that you did something wrong that ticked your friend off. As a result, they don't want to call anymore because they don't want to be your friend anymore. And maybe you even ask, "What did I do?" That painful narrative then causes you to behave differently with your friend in response to this perceived slight. You'll shift from being sad to angry. Afterwards, you may get defensive or less caring in order to protect yourself. These thoughts then translate to physical actions when you stop calling and engaging with said friend. That's painful, isn't it?

But what if you stopped and took a moment to ask: "Is that really what's happening? Am I perpetuating this story by behaving in this way?" By taking your friend's behavior personally, you're creating from a space of pain instead of a space of possibility that maybe your friend has been really busy and hasn't had a chance to call you. What if you quieted your ego and realized that you haven't done anything wrong at all against your friend? That sometimes life just gets in the way, and later, when you reconnect with said friend, their perspective might be that they stopped calling because you stopped calling?

Why do interpersonal events like this have to immediately mean what our egos and insecurities say first? Why do we make everything, including other people's behavior, about us? By taking moments like this personally, you are hurting not only yourself and your relationships with others, but truly stopping yourself from being the best of yourself. To truly be the best of yourself, you can learn to balance your insecurities and quiet the ego from creating damaging stories from other people's actions. Again, what people do is not about you.

Dramas in life perpetuate in the mind as they are psychological. It is our choice to perceive and focus upon, and to "keep alive" these things. Disagreements, conflict, fighting, all start in the mind and are kept going there. It's our personal mind that can be at peace, if we choose it to be that way.

Being the best of yourself also means being able to not take what the universe puts out personally. More importantly, it's being able to understand our own role in what we attract into our lives from the universe and how to act in spirit. There are always going to be ups and downs in our lives because our lives are full of multiple relationships and continuous outside circumstances. Life is always happening all around us. But as I have said before, a circumstance simply IS. It is not good or bad; it is our mind that tells us so. What matters is how we respond or react to these things. Our reactions to life are our greatest teachers.

You'll see over and over that your brain will create false or neurotic stories of how an event is unfolding, and then you'll talk to the other person (or people) involved and they will have a completely different take on what's actually happening. Your brain is working overtime to create these narratives because it's working from your own perspective, through your own eyes and from the standpoint of who you are. *You* are the cause to *your effect;* things don't just happen to you by accident. Events and conflicts don't just occur; you attract them through your own experience and through your own life. Next time, try to catch yourself before you take something personally and ask yourself: "What within me asked for this?" You'll be able to locate what idea or belief system within you needs your attention and work.

The idea you have of yourself is so important because if you are constantly a person who takes things personally, then it's going to change the fabric of the life you create. If you are constantly acting from a place of being offended and taking things personally, it's most likely because you're lacking in self-confidence and self-worth. When the idea you have of yourself is so low, it's very easy to think that everything happening is about you.

Every action has a reaction, and when you take something personally, you're reacting from that place. You're making a decision or taking action from a place of not being your best self. This creates a cause and effect where, if you're expressing life from a place of self-consciousness, lack or even poor self-worth, you're attracting more of the same. Usually, when you are in this low vibrational space, you're creating negative energy that perpetuates the actual fear you're acting from.

For example, I know someone who had a consistent friend group that lasted for years. The people in the group enjoyed many of the same activities and hobbies and looked forward to spending time together. Soon, a new person was introduced into the group, and the person I knew in the group felt threatened. Suddenly, this person felt like they weren't good enough to hang out with this friend group anymore. This belief bled into how this person started to live and act. They started to recede and exile themselves from the group. They stopped calling and making plans with said group. Soon enough, the group returned the behavior in kind. On top of taking the new person's arrival to the group personally and feeling threatened, this person then took the group's response to their behavior personally as well! This person failed to realize that because she took it personally, she put that energy out there and the group responded in kind to what she was putting out. When we react from our limitations within our own consciousness, we create the very scenario we feared.

I have learned that some relationships change and others end. My decision to simply allow both to be the case and not apply a personal meaning to it has led to significant peace of mind. I don't have to be hurt, I don't have to be angry, and I don't have to know why the relationship changed. All I need to know is that it did and there must be a good reason for it. Thank the universe and move on. We have to learn to move forward without taking it personally. Otherwise, we're stuck in the same story our brain and ego are creating and damaging our potential to be the best of ourselves.

Life, even with all the ups and downs and changes, is dependent on the choices and decisions we make. If we are acting out of a place of insecurity and fear because we're taking something personal, we are not giving ourselves the best possible options and choices. From the example above, we can see how damaging our choices can be if we are only acting out of that space of lack. But what if you were a stronger, more confident person? What would you believe? If you were secure in yourself and had a lot of self-love, what would you say? What kind of choices would you be allowing yourself to take?

This requires a paradigm shift to make the decision to see what things could be and their potential, rather than what you think they are. Remember, you're seeing through your own personal lens, so the more your lens is geared towards knowing yourself and abundance, the more you can open yourself up to potential. Our lens also comes through your consciousness, so you must think through what obstacles are causing you to impose a limited vision of yourself out into the world.

I want to be clear: I'm not saying you should be okay with being disrespected or being treated as a doormat. Unfortunately, there may be people in your life who will not treat you kindly or with respect. What I'm asking you to do is to check in with yourself and how you can be within your spirit and understand that any lack of kindness, disrespect, or mistreatment you experience from someone else is a reflection of their consciousness and the limitations within. Most importantly (and challenging) is then being able to respond to unkindness and mistreatment with compassion and leave them with the impression that they are being elevated. Don't lower your value because someone else doesn't see it.

Every time a situation occurs when someone disrespects you, ask yourself, how have I reflected this? It could be you are asking for better relationships so you are shown the ones that aren't serving you. It could be you have accepted this treatment in the past, and this harsher treatment is happening so you finally stop accepting it and move on!

Too often we conflate the belief that someone behaves in a certain way because it's a reflection of OUR worth. "I'm not good enough because I'm ugly/short/not smart (insert any other kind of insecurity you struggle with)." But it doesn't mean that at all, and it's important to understand that people's behaviors or actions are not about you.

When I was in my twenties and dating, if someone didn't want to see me anymore, I took it extremely personally! I would always wonder: "What did I do wrong? How was I not good enough?" If that person didn't like me, I made it out to be because I was less than in some capacity. Truthfully, you're not meant to engage with every single person that likes you, and guess what, not every single person is going to like you! And in turn, you're not going to like every single person you meet or date either. Nor can dating be a solution for certain internal insecurities and fears we still need to iron out. Instead of needing to be liked or needing to be loved no matter what by everyone we date, what stops us from just accepting that we're just not in alignment with people? And that's okay!

I've had people leave my life in professional and personal capacities. The first time someone left my business, she was in a very important leadership role in my organization and had been with me from the beginning. She left in a way that was loud and created a lot of conflict. At that time, I made it all about me. My feelings were hurt. I felt disrespected, and I made it out to be about something I did. I felt shame and guilt. I also felt like I had been wronged and that she was the one wronging me.

In truth, this whole emotional experience was actually a powerful lesson. I realized I was making it all about me and my need to be right, to be loved, to be worthy, and needing people to think that I'm a good person. At the time, wanting to be seen as a good person meant a lot to me, and I knew this needed to be examined. Why did this happen? Did I think I wasn't a good person? Did I not think I was kind? Did I give enough? Was I grateful enough? What was it within me that I was reacting to in such a way? That situation was a gift because it showed me that I had work to do on myself and my consciousness. I learned that any time I have hurt feelings and feel disrespected or disappointed, I have to forgive myself and take myself out of the equation when my ego is hurting. Why do I need to be liked? This question is very powerful and can help you move out of your ego and back into your spirit.

Elevating to the best of yourself is a strategy and toolkit on how to become more resilient in life. It's a way to become the best version of yourself that isn't taken down as much by the experiences or turbulence of life. This is how you create the permanence that'll help you stay on course to accomplish your goals and dreams and stay strong so the hiccups of life don't throw you off course.

The old me got thrown off course all the time by smaller emotional turbulences, especially the inner perspectives and fears that were being mirrored back to me by other people. Here's an example.

Back when I started my business in January 2020, I got into a really big, defining argument with my dad. He was taking me to the airport so I could fly to Los Angeles to attend Bob Proctor's Paradigm Shift. When we parked, he took it upon himself to tell me how concerned he was that I was becoming a "mindset coach." He felt it was too risky. In my dad's eyes, I had said goodbye to my nursing career and to the safety of my pension, benefits, and sustainable pay. Essentially, I was throwing away my future security. Was this what I should be doing? This argument happened right when I was the most inspired in my career, so I was lit up with excitement before we had this crushing conversation. I was pissed. I was so mad. I told him that I couldn't believe he was saying this, right now, as I was on my way to launch my business. I was the happiest I had ever been in my life, and here was my dad, leaving me crestfallen.

That Kathleen took it personally. This was another reason I wasn't good enough and my own dad didn't believe in me. This argument was reinforcing that insecurity I had that I wasn't smart enough or successful enough to take this risk. Understandably, I resented him for it. But I'm a different Kathleen today. I look at him and know that my dad had no malicious intent. He was a father with a daughter who was doing something he didn't really believe in at that time because he couldn't see past that $100K a year mark to that multi-million dollar business I had planned for. It's not like he was going to tell me to NOT go after my dreams, but he was a father who was worried, and I took it the other way because I was seeing it through the lens of my insecurities. I took this argument personally because I wasn't believing in myself, and I was a little worried too. My dad just said what I was thinking, and it made me mad. He was a reflection of what I was going through internally.

But because he said those things, I got to step into a different version of myself because he made me mad. I was driven to prove him (and myself!) wrong, and I did. I got the opportunity to tell him, and myself, that this wasn't a risk but a done deal! It solidified my belief in me. Now, my dad works in my business. Here's a full circle moment: three years after that pivotal argument at the airport where my dad called me crazy for taking this risk, my father and I are both in Los Angeles now, and my dad is mediating, visualizing, and working in my business. Not only is he working for me, making an income, but we're going on hikes, eating beautiful dinners, and living our best lives together.

While this story has a happy ending, it's important to note that my father's perception was coming from his consciousness. When I chose to take his perception and take it as my own truth to my own insecurities, I was lowering my own vibrational state to match him. When people are at a lower level of awareness, don't know themselves as well as they could, and are not emotionally regulated, they will not see the world in the way that you see it because they can't understand it. This could make you, if you're at a higher level of awareness, feel wrong or conflicted. But you at your higher level of awareness will never make someone at a lower level feel or be wrong. Do you feel that difference? Being at a higher level of awareness always invites the lower level friend, partner, family member, etc., to elevate themselves. That's why when someone, usually on a lower level of awareness (not less than), is trying to make me wrong, the last thing I want to do (or feel called to do) is make them wrong back. Staying in my integrity and authenticity is a big enough invite for others to elevate and do the same.

If you continue to take things personally, you're forfeiting your own peace of mind. We all think we want influence, money and success, but what we all want at the end of every day is peace of mind. We all want to live a great life, but we don't want to be in a state of suffering or bondage within our own minds. Peace of mind is easy and giving; it opens you up to allow for more love, more joy, more abundance, and more gratitude. To achieve peace of mind means you must let go of the things that are limiting you and holding you to an old version of yourself. Peace of mind is found in the surrender. Taking things personally is one of those anchors holding you down and causing you to choose unnecessary suffering.

One way I know I have peace of mind is when I take inventory and stock of my life right before I go to sleep. An older version of me would lay in bed thinking of all the things I did wrong that day, or the things I meant to do but didn't. I'd fixate on the conflict in my life or my stresses around my old nursing job. Peace of mind means that now I lay in bed and don't have to think about any of those things. I'm not thinking about the regrets I have or ruminating on the mistakes I've made in life. It's about going to bed and thinking about how amazing today was, how great life is, and how I'm looking forward to tomorrow.

Peace OF *mind* IS FOUND IN THE *surrender.*

The kind of life I want to live is one where I fall asleep at night in a state of rest and relaxation and wake up excited for the next day, grateful that I have it. If you're taking things personal, you're going to be self-critical, self-judgmental, and always wondering, *how can I* not *do that tomorrow?* Or you're going to believe that's just the way you are and you're doomed to repeat another anxiety-inducing day trapped in the suffering of your own thinking. Just today on one of my teaching calls, a student noted that she now goes to bed in gratitude every night. Now that is peace.

If you are in a sales position, I would consider this example. Is the sale you are making about you or about the person being sold to? My greatest successes have come when I do not make it about me, or make it personal. When I want to close a sale because I want to feel good, I want the feedback on my sales ability, or I want the commission, I have just made it personal. So, when someone doesn't buy what you are selling, you think you failed, your energy drops, and you feel deflated. But what's really happened is that you have put your feelings of fulfillment first before helping that person. I love to consider a sale with no gain to myself whatsoever. What would that be like? This feeling is powerful and it attracts. The other repels. The commission or sense of accomplishment becomes a bonus after helping someone fulfill a need.

Neutrality is a healthy place to exist in and something to practice daily. Neutrality is actually how we can go from having "bad days" to just days, or even "good days" all the time. Nothing is good or bad until we say it is so. Every event, experience, or thing that happens in your life isn't anything until you give it meaning, and the meaning you give it determines the outcome of that event. Everything, even your day, is based on the way you are reacting to what's happening.

If something happens, and you say it's bad, you just gave the event a bad meaning, which in turn makes you feel bad, creating a ripple effect. And you then attract more of the same feeling. The law is never wrong.

Staying neutral to experiences creates peace of mind. When someone leaves your life, that's just the event; it's not good or bad. It doesn't have a good/bad meaning until we filter it through our perception, which again is connected to our self-awareness.

So what do we do in these cases? I would encourage you to be accepting of events and experiences as they are and move on, allowing yourself to find a new person for the job, create space for newer better aligned relationships, or to allow for a better version of yourself. Release the judgements you have of yourself, of others, of the world, and go into a state of gratitude and decide how you want your tomorrow to be…and stop taking it all so personally!

CHAPTER 14:
Journal Prompts

Reflecting on the power of perception: Consider the statement, "Our feelings get hurt because we choose to perceive whatever was said in a certain way with a meaning that hurts our feelings, ego, and sense of self." Explore instances when you have experienced hurt feelings based on your interpretation of someone's words or actions. How can you become more aware of your own perception filters and the meanings you assign to situations? Reflect on strategies to cultivate a more objective and resilient mindset that is less prone to being hurt by external factors.

Navigating obstacles on the path to self-improvement: Reflect on the statement, "I firmly believe that the root of many obstacles you'll encounter in life exists to keep you from being the best of yourself." Identify obstacles or challenges you have faced on your personal growth journey. How have these obstacles tested your commitment and determination to become the best version of yourself? Reflect on the lessons and insights gained from overcoming these obstacles. How can you approach future challenges with a mindset focused on growth and self-improvement?

Building resilience and inner alignment: Consider the statement, "How can we ensure that we are right in spirit to make these tough calls? How can we make sure we're centered enough with ourselves not to get thrown off course when these things happen?" Reflect on situations in your life when external events or circumstances have caused disruption or disappointment. How did these experiences impact your inner alignment and decision-making process? Explore practices and strategies to help you build resilience and maintain a centered state of mind amidst challenges and unexpected changes. How can you cultivate self-awareness, inner strength, and emotional balance to navigate tough decisions and remain on course toward becoming the best version of yourself?

CHAPTER **FIFTEEN:**

Attraction Based On You

We cannot talk about becoming the best of
ourselves without discussing attraction.

When I teach the law of vibration, and the secondary law of attraction, I focus on how it enables us to create our lives based on who we are *at that moment*. This means that what we are attracting is a direct read on who we are and what we believe about ourselves at that point in time. Vibration is described using feeling words, so how you feel about you today is your point of attraction for tomorrow. The simplest way to describe this is to discuss the feeling of success versus the feeling of failure. We can easily see how those two would feel for us. Now, which do you resonate with most? Which do you feel most of the time? Are you feeling like a success and thus attracting more, or are you feeling like you haven't done enough yet and attracting from there?

Seeing as we are meant to evolve and push past the limits of ourselves, it's natural that some of the things or people we attracted to us in the past are no longer relevant to who we are in our elevated form. The best of yourself deserves and attracts only the <u>best</u>.

For example, what happens many times after people start a mentorship with me is that they find their perspective on their longstanding relationships changes. As they become the best of themselves, inevitably their confidence rises, they believe in themselves more, and they light up as they start to elevate in their awareness and growth. Soon, they'll start to notice that the people in their lives do not match their newfound vibration or awareness. Often, they begin to describe people in their lives as negative. I notice they begin to get activated because they feel as though they have released themselves from negativity, thus they don't want to be pulled back down. What is really happening here is a misalignment of vibrations. This misalignment with old friends and partners, business or romantic, often leaves them feeling conflicted about leaving or moving on. Usually one of two things occurs: my clients either help these people elevate or they move on.

One thing is always clear though and important to remember as you become the best of yourself: you attracted everyone that is in your life to you by who you believed you were in that moment. But now you've changed. You're a different version of yourself, and what you attracted twenty years ago will be completely different from what you attract into your life today. As you elevate, you will become very aware of how different those around you now are, but they are not, you are and now you perceive them differently. What used to be your normal, gossiping, complaining, venting, will now bother you as you no longer want to engage in unproductive behavior. My best piece of advice is to have compassion, to encourage your loved ones, to help them elevate, to see how you want them to be, and to be the light for them. You'd be surprised how many people rise up to meet the challenge and elevate themselves when a loved and/or trusted friend is evolving to a better version of themselves.

I BELIEVE MY *power* CAN HELP THEM SEE *their own*.

Sometimes, my clients have to terminate these relationships and move on. If folks aren't going to rise or change to be the best of themselves while you really want to be the best of yourself, then what is keeping that relationship in your life worthwhile? Is that a dynamic you really want to hold space for while all these amazing changes and experiences are happening? I'm not telling you to rid yourself of people in your life, but I am telling you to ask yourself the question: *Is this somebody I still want to have around me? Do they add to my life positively? Do I love them and myself unconditionally?*

Not everyone has the power to impact you negatively. I believe that my own light is so bright and strong that negative people cannot impact me negatively. This was not always what I believed, but it is a thought I nurtured and convinced myself of. Understandably, not everyone believes this at this moment. So, if you are still allowing people outside of you to impact inside of you, maybe ask yourself why?

I also believe that because my light is so bright, I can be the light for others, so I hold space for others to expand and grow. I'm not going to give up on them or walk away from them, but I'm going to give them the opportunity in their own time to elevate and become the best version of themselves that they're happy with. I always hold the image of how I would like them to be. I believe my power can help them see their own.

In the last chapter, we talked about a specific argument with my dad and how within three years, he went from doubting my whole business to working for my business. He's always reading and researching for the business. He listens, meditates, and/or visualizes with the team and is moving into his feminine energy. I didn't have to force him or ask him to do it. I simply held space for him while being myself and supported him as he grew at his own pace. I believe we can hold this space for those we care about most.

In the law of vibration, everything is an energetic motion because energy is in motion all the time. We're actually describing our vibrational state all the time. Any time we use feeling words or start a sentence with, "I feel," we're describing our vibrational state at that point in time. When we say, "I am sad," we are describing a vibration that is low and slow. When we say, "I am happy," we are describing a vibration that is high and fast.

Enlightenment is a pretty high and elevated vibration and space. It's a vibrational state that says, "Nothing can phase me." The world is happening around you and it's not bothering you. It means being at a very specific vibrational state. But so is guilt, shame, and fear—they are different vibrational states. It's important to understand that we are always at a frequency of vibration, like a radio station we are tuned into, which then determines what our magnet will draw to us. We're always attracting based on the state we're in.

The law of vibration says we are always in motion, and thus we always have a vibration. The law of attraction, the secondary law, says there is always a point of attraction based on our emotional state. Not only does your in moment emotion make a difference but more so, the emotional conception of the self. How you see you has a feeling, and it attracts or repels. This is why we attract people who are similar to us, or people who have the same fears and insecurities as us. It can also mean attracting people with the same goals, ambitions, and dreams if we're both at the same frequency.

In business, it's the same way. You attract people who want to work with you and who are similar to you. It's about managing your emotional regulation to know the point of attraction that you're in so that your magnet is powerful and bringing you everything you want instead of everything you don't want. Finding a way to be positive and to hold yourself in a positive light is so crucial to attracting the best opportunities and people toward you. It doesn't mean always being happy. It means you believe you are strong, powerful, and confident even though you may have unhappy moments. It's also paying attention to your dominant feeling, not policing every thought and every feeling every day. I ask myself before I drift off to sleep, *what was my dominant feeling today?*

IT'S ABOUT MANAGING YOUR EMOTIONAL REGULATION TO *know* THE POINT OF *attraction* THAT YOU'RE IN SO THAT YOUR MAGNET IS *powerful* AND BRINGING YOU *everything you want* INSTEAD OF EVERYTHING YOU DON'T WANT.

There's a difference between artificial and intentional positivity. Some people will pretend to be happy. When you're faking positivity, your point of attraction is not going to be happiness, nor will the vibration you're on emit happiness. When you're faking a mindset, it's usually to soothe an insecurity or fear, and that insecurity or fear will be what you attract and vibrate. It's about your subconscious pattern and program and who you are. The feeling of you matters.

When you see yourself as only moderately successful, there's an emotional component that has an attractive magnetism to similar mindsets and opportunities. So you will attract things that will keep you moderately successful. If you see yourself as a badass CEO, entrepreneur, or leader, there's an emotional conception of that, so the point of attraction is going to be different. You're going to attract different opportunities when you think you're just moderately successful versus when you think of yourself as a badass entrepreneur.

Even in sales, there is a different feeling and point of attraction for somebody who thinks they are okay at sales, or someone who is learning to be better at sales, versus someone who believes they are a sales shark. It's not like you need to go and take a course on how to be the best salesperson, but you do need to vibrate already believing yourself to be an incredible salesperson. Pretending or faking these mindsets, beliefs, or what you truly want is just a bandage hiding some inner work or fear you need to work on. The way you see yourself matters, but especially how you feel about yourself. Once you truly believe you are what you seek to be, you will see that show up in your physical world, it's universal law.

Since we attract positive, neutral, and negative experiences and people to us depending on our own vibration, it's important to learn how to determine what you're attracting will work for you or against you.

Let's say you're working with a company you thought was a good fit. You two were in alignment when you first met. However, as time passes, maybe you realize you're actually not a great fit and the business opportunity is not quite what you'd hoped it would be. How can you navigate that you attracted something that wasn't great for you in the long run?

Perhaps it is that the person that you were four months ago when this hypothetical meeting with the company happened attracted this company to you. You attracted this company and opportunity based on who you were at that point in time. Since you've gotten into the company, you've shifted, you've changed, and your confidence has grown. What you're willing to accept and not accept has changed. So, had you not joined this business opportunity, you would not have known what you really wanted. So attracting this was valuable, especially in your attraction of what is to come next.

Instead of getting upset with yourself or mad at yourself for thinking you made a mistake, you can take it as a lesson, understanding that everything is a learning process. Every relationship is a learning opportunity. You have learned through this experience exactly the type of people you want to work with and exactly the kind of business you want to do and how.

Sometimes this means ending certain jobs or opportunities with grace and authenticity, or sitting down to rehash if you still have any compatible goals or strategies with this company to get where you want. Just like in personal relationships, these differences can sometimes be an opportunity to be a light for another person or business to elevate themselves. No matter what happens, with a newfound awareness and learning of self, you can keep yourself grounded in grace, integrity, and authenticity.

You can have these areas or moments of enlightenment happen anywhere or at any time. You can change just by journaling or by taking a course. When I decided to step into the person I truly wanted to be and desired, that meant making a physical decision that changed the physical location I was in. This decision helped me rise in my consciousness. I want to stress that this mindset change wasn't because of the physical location. itself; it was because I was ready and willing to take the step to be the kind of person I saw and desired within myself. This is ultimately how attraction works. You have to see yourself in the way you want to be in order to take the steps necessary to bring that version of yourself to life. It's important to check in with the current version of yourself to decide if it's who you want to be. Then, see yourself in the way you want to be to attract better opportunities, people, and experiences.

If you're reading this book, you already want more out of life. While you might only see one step ahead right now, I want you to use this book to see twenty steps ahead and take all those twenty steps. What if you could have more? What if you could elevate even further? What if you could do more? There are always higher levels of every single experience. There are higher levels of love than any of us have ever experienced. There are higher levels of gratitude than any of us have ever experienced. There are higher levels of wealth and abundance, peace and serenity, and they are all waiting for you if that's what you want. It's in the attainment of the experience of these higher levels that we have the opportunity to make our experiences better and better.

I have learned that I desire the experience of attaining my goals rather than having people tell me I'm great or validating that. It's about not leaving this life feeling like I only measured up to someone else's expectations or goals of me, but it's about using my own metric of success. Ultimately, this is about releasing the need to be validated, releasing the need to be loved, and releasing the need to be told that I made a difference by other people and knowing inherently, on my own, I am worthy, deserving, and have done all those things. It's about experiencing life in a different way in the most positive possible way for me so that I can teach people how to do it themselves.

To accomplish this for yourself, it's important to understand that you are the one resisting your leveling up. You aren't blocked or obstructed by anything.

Even the word *block* implies there's something in your way, something you have to overcome, or some kind of hurdle. In truth, it's your own resistance that's holding you back. When I use the word *resistance*, it simply means you are not open to receive. By allowing it in, you can have it.

For example, someone could desire wealth but they're having trouble getting there because they are resisting it by choosing lack and limitation. They are not *blocked* by wealth; wealth is not something to overcome. Focusing on what you lack and your limitations will always ensure you won't get to where you want to go. What if you want more success but you're resisting? How do you know you're resisting? Because you don't have it and aren't allowing it in.

The resistance comes from limitations you have within yourself, such as your fears and insecurities. The more limitations we remove, the more resistance we remove, the more we allow ourselves to let in abundance, success, wealth, and goals. It's less about *creating* a newer version of you, and more about allowing a stronger version of you to step forward that's always existed. How can we let go of the lies and programming we've held onto that holds us back? How can we allow that version to shine through?

We have to ask ourselves, *if I want more of X, what is the Y that's giving me resistance?* The more we realize what is holding us back, the more we can see the full, complete version of ourselves that exists and step forward into our abundant futures. How much more of what I want am I willing to allow in? By "being" it, we match its vibration and we allow. Shift into the feeling of what you'd love and you're golden.

FINDING A WAY TO BE
POSITIVE AND TO HOLD
yourself
IN A POSITIVE LIGHT
IS SO CRUCIAL TO
ATTRACTING THE BEST
opportunities
AND PEOPLE
TOWARD YOU.

CHAPTER 15:
Journal Prompts

Reflecting on the evolution of attraction: Consider the statement, "When I focus on the law of attraction, I focus on how it enables us to create our lives based on who we are at that moment." Reflect on moments in your life when you have witnessed the power of attraction aligning with your beliefs and self-perception. How have your desires and manifestations shifted as you have grown and evolved into your best self? What insights can you gain from this realization? How can you intentionally attract experiences and relationships that are in alignment with your current state of being?

Embracing the power of self-belief in the law of attraction: Reflect on the statement, "What we are attracting is a direct read on who we are and what we believe about ourselves at that point in time." Reflect on moments when your beliefs about yourself have influenced the outcomes and opportunities that have come your way. How can you strengthen and expand your self-belief to attract experiences that are in alignment with your best self? What practices or affirmations can you incorporate into your daily life to reinforce positive self-beliefs and attract desired outcomes?

Aligning with your higher self through intentional attraction: Consider the statement, "Seeing as we are always evolving and pushing to be our best selves, it's natural that some of the things or people we attracted to us in the past are no longer relevant to who we are in our higher form." Reflect on the concept of alignment with your higher self and its role in the Law of Attraction. How can you intentionally release and let go of experiences, things, or people that no longer serve your growth and alignment with your higher self? How can you consciously attract experiences and individuals that support your journey of becoming your best self?

CHAPTER **SIXTEEN:**

Healing the Self

When I first started learning about the law of attraction, and the power of the mind, I became aware that the subconscious mind is programmed through feeling. Any emotion you feel or experience sends a message to the subconscious mind and impresses itself upon it to create a pattern. I realized that the events, experiences, people, and fears you emotionalize become your patterns and your programs. Essentially, these become our habits, automatic reactions to future events that the mind thinks are similar. Being new to my journey, I was determined to use this information to unlock how to control my emotions versus keeping my emotions from controlling me. Still, I had so much to learn.

In my early days, and armed with this knowledge, I wanted to make sure that I was feeling the most productive emotions every day to ensure that I was attracting the right people, opportunities, and experiences that would add positively to my life. I wanted to be happy, in joy and gratitude all the time, and therefore, I fought against feeling negative emotions because I didn't want them to impress themselves upon my subconscious mind. My goal was to create positive and empowering patterns and programs and not limiting ones like I had before. I started to discipline and regulate my emotions. I had heard somewhere that seventeen seconds in an emotion sets it into the subconscious mind, so I got quick at replacing my emotional state.

This meant that I started paying attention to what feeling I was in and to actively swap the feeling if it wasn't in line with the things I wanted to attract. For example, if I didn't want my point of attraction to come from frustration, and if I felt frustrated, I would switch my emotion by replacing it with the opposite feeling. I became really good at avoiding negative feelings and leaning into just disciplining my feelings, making sure they were as "good" as possible. Did that process help me manifest? Absolutely. Because I was able to change my physical world through changing my emotional internal state, I attracted money and powerful people, and I became more magnetic. I got the business I wanted. My life was aligning itself with my perfect vision. After two years of doing this, deeper emotional experiences occurred within me that made me reevaluate my entire process.

In February 2022, I separated from my husband. I moved out of the family house into a home by myself that I rented for six months. My daughters came to stay with me every other week, so we were not a family living full-time together anymore, and this change was drastic. This was all new and became a huge deviation from the way I had been living. As negative feelings (sadness, loneliness, fear, insecurity) arose, I told myself that I was okay, that I was fine, that I was strong, that maybe this was an opportunity to put time into my own development. I had a list of books I wanted to read and a new motivation to walk every day and to exercise. Not soon after, several members of my company, who I also felt were dear friends, left and started a company together with a similar business model to my own. The outside world was getting louder, and it was getting harder and harder not to react.

These events were extremely emotional, but I believed I was stronger than this negativity. My response was to push these feelings down and instead switch them with their opposite feeling. I kept telling myself that I was okay, that I was stronger than this. My go-to mantra was: *You've got this, Kathleen.*

By April, it all caught up with me. I was so good at distracting myself with work and travel that I honestly was not "feeling" too much. I went from Toronto to New York to Toronto to Austin and ended up getting a cold. While in Texas, I got diagnosed with walking pneumonia and was prescribed antibiotics. I had this severe pain in the right side of my upper back, and I assumed it was a pulled muscle from all the coughing. My dad flew to Texas to help bring me to Florida where my entire family was before I was set to run my very first retreat in the Bahamas. The pain got worse day after day, and I ended up going back to the doctor and was sent to the hospital with fluid on my right lung. I spent a few days in the Fort Lauderdale Hospital where they were treating me with IV antibiotics and considering whether to drain the lung. I went in for the draining procedure and they did an ultrasound, which revealed the fluid was almost gone, so they ended up releasing me from the hospital with antibiotics and a few painkillers.

I flew to the Bahamas with my mom and spent three days rotating between sleeping and teaching. Over those days, I progressively got worse, ran out of painkillers, and my mom ended up packing all our stuff, booked a private plane to Miami, and woke me telling me we were going to the hospital. She took matters into her own hands and saved my life.

No more than 24 hours later, I was having lung surgery to release my right lung from infection. My lung was completely collapsed and trapped and was the size of a coin. I had developed four empyemas (fluid-filled infection pockets) surrounding the entire right lung, and the aggressive infection had taken over. My kidney function was decreasing every day, and there was no other way to fix it all then major surgery. I ended up in the ICU for a short time, spent over a week in the hospital, and recovered in a hotel room in Miami for another three weeks, unable to fly home to see my daughters until I was medically safe to do so.

I was completely helpless and felt totally debilitated. The disease rendered me immobile. I was at the mercy of modern medicine. My 3D world was loud, painful, and very emotional. I remember sitting in the hospital room crying. I couldn't stop the emotions from flooding out of me, which was a good thing I would soon realize. What I didn't know yet was that my physical disease was just a physical expression of the internal disease that I was carrying.

Soon after my surgery, I found out that the spiritual meaning of pneumonia is <u>repressed grief</u>. Given the upheaval I'd just experienced, this struck me very profoundly. Did I grieve the recent losses of my old life? Of my old self? Of the friendships lost, the relationship that had changed? I understood immediately that I hadn't allowed myself to feel and heal from so many hard and emotional events in my life: my separation, the changing family dynamic, my daughters being away from me, the loss of my team. All these experiences were deeply hurtful. What was worse is that I didn't give myself an opportunity to feel <u>any</u> of that. I hadn't debriefed what had happened or sat in my sadness. Early-manifesting Kathleen's motto was: *You've got this, Kathleen.* Over a year later, the woman I am now is saying that it's pivotal to instead experience the fullness of your emotional state.

By allowing yourself to feel the full experience of your emotional state, you can ask yourself why you're feeling that particular emotion and attempt to heal it. Today's, Kathleen's motto is: *Feel it to heal it.* Only after feeling an emotion can you ask yourself for vital information about the feeling and its roots. Pushing away a feeling to swap it out—much like what I was doing before—was robbing me of getting to know myself better and understanding what was going on internally. It was also just leaving the energy stored in my body.

Feeling the feeling allowed me to ask the following questions:

What is the story I'm telling myself? Is this what I want this story to be?

What's my perception here? Is there some neutrality I can gain?

How am I framing this? Can I reframe this to be more productive?

Can my emotions change? Is what I'm going through a cathartic release of that emotion? Could feeling this emotion and the awareness of it be the best way to release it?

IT'S ALSO OKAY TO *grieve* PAST VERSIONS OF *yourself* AS YOU'RE *elevating* AND GROWING.

That last question was new for me at the time. I now find it to be integral. I truly had to embody and practice that it was okay for me to feel negative feelings and grieve all the changes in my life. It's okay to feel sad. It's okay to grieve. It's okay to recognize that your world is changing. It's also okay to grieve past versions of yourself as you're elevating and growing. Most people forget to allow themselves the grace to do so.

When we talk about becoming the best of ourselves and elevating to an elevated version of ourselves, we're leaving behind our old selves (the ones we used to think we were). Of course, there will be conflicting emotions associated with that. Sometimes you're going to want to hang onto that past version of yourself because it's safe and comfortable. Sometimes you're going to want to judge or downplay a past version of yourself because you're embarrassed or ashamed. With my clients and in my classes, I encourage people NOT to do that and instead to extend gratitude to your past versions. That past version you're embarrassed by got you to where you are today. That version of you was necessary in order to get to this stronger, better version of you. Be thankful. It's okay to break away from people, experiences, or things that are no longer aligned or relevant with your best self. Still, it's important to remain in a state of gratitude and respect that all these things helped get you to where you are today.

I changed my world around when I let myself grieve the entire experience. I processed all of it, from the separation to the business affairs to the surgery. I let myself grieve all the way back to past versions of my life when I worked as a nurse. This was a very important part of my life. There are so many parts of the old Kathleen that are still here. It's okay to be sad that a part of you isn't there anymore because you need to move onto your next chapter. Emotional regulation, I learned, isn't about switching your emotions; it's about becoming aware of your emotions, allowing the emotions to show up, allowing the experience of the emotion to occur, and then being able to work through it and heal from it. Only then can you move onto better and more productive emotions.

I realized that my old method of swapping feelings when they became negative meant that I was not always authentically myself. To stay aligned with my belief system and with the paradigms of how I see myself, I realized that feeling through my emotions was more aligned with living my life with integrity and authenticity. Knowing this, I encourage all my students, friends, and family to feel ALL the emotions—just don't sit in them.

There's a difference between feeling through an emotion and just sitting and dwelling on an emotion. In Chapters 14 and 15, we talked about how a feeling, an emotion, is energy. Feelings and emotions describe the energy or vibrational state we're in. When we change moods or emotions, we're actually saying there's a change in our energy. We've shifted into a different energy or vibration. That energy is in your body. It's happening. I want us to allow that feeling to move through you and not get stuck in you. Because I didn't allow myself to grieve, I let that energy get stuck and get repressed within me. How it expressed itself was as a disease that took over my body only after it became stuck in my mind. I don't want you to sit in the energy of an emotion; I want you to let it move through you so you can turn it into a productive experience or into a new productive vibration.

Sometimes, modern culture makes that difficult. For example, when we go through a breakup, we're encouraged to lean into the stressful experience of getting rejected. We are told to soak in our sadness or guilt by binging on sad love songs, depressing movies, and our favorite ice cream. While that may feel good in the moment, it's ultimately unproductive. You're amplifying the feeling and causing yourself to re-experience it over and over as a raw emotion rather than learning from it and getting in closer contact with yourself. In situations like these, we need to find ways to release that emotion's energy in a productive way after we've felt it all. It's about letting the wound heal without any lasting complications.

LET IT MOVE
THROUGH YOU
SO YOU CAN
TURN IT INTO
A PRODUCTIVE
experience
OR INTO A NEW
PRODUCTIVE
vibration.

The body remembers. While all the emotional experiences I went through in 2022 were hard, my health crisis alone was particularly taxing on my body. While the experience itself was very unpleasant, I am not traumatized because I found ways to resolve my emotions and heal. Still, my body remembers the stress it went through, which only makes me human. Even as I'm writing this chapter and talking about it, my throat is tight and my voice cracks. The old Kathleen wants to not talk about it and to hold it all in. Despite this, the new Kathleen knows that it helps to talk through these events and experiences with trusted advisors or with myself. What's really important here is journaling. Journaling allows me to be reflective and to observe and notate what's happening and what I'm experiencing and what I'm feeling as a mindfulness exercise.

By talking about my surgery, I feel the emotion as the experience floods back. I recall being helpless and in extreme pain, not being able to move, and being so very sad. People don't mention this often, but the emotional knife related to surgery is just as sharp and long-lasting as the physical knife; unfortunately, people only focus on the physical cutting, not the emotional. I remember after my surgery I felt so low. This dark cloud floated over me. I couldn't get out of my rut for nearly six weeks.

Journaling allowed me to record all this and see my patterns because immediately after my dark cloud left, I felt immensely happy. Though I wish I could go back in time and tell the old Kathleen that she would return to living her best life, I'm grateful for the opportunity to take my feelings seriously and to study them as a way to know myself deeper and to truly put my belief systems to the test. Overall, emotional journaling is an excellent way to talk to yourself and get necessary perspective on your situation.

When journaling, the first question you want to ask is, "What am I feeling in this moment?" Did you notice an energetic drop or an emotional impact?

For me, I'll notice it and say or write: "Why do I want to cry right now?"

Then I work backwards and ask: "What happened to get me to that feeling? Was it something someone said? Did I see something? What is the event or situation? What is my story about this event? Is that story true? Is it real? Does this really mean x or that I am actually y? Why do I need to feel/recreate this fear? What's the wound I need to heal?"

All these answers make you more intentional about your perspective and find the source of the issue as well as the solution.

Sometimes, we need an outside perspective when we need to heal out of a feeling. If you're going to engage someone else in your healing process, you're going to want to make sure it's someone who is going to promote your healing instead of perpetuating the same story of suffering you're already stuck in.

For example, let's say you just went through an awful breakup where you found out the person who was supposed to be your partner cheated on you. You're absolutely heartbroken. In this situation, a lot of us turn to our parents for advice or support. Let's say your mother is a trusted confidant and she's more than happy to be your support system during this time… except, instead of helping you heal, she's helping you perpetuate the story you keep telling yourself. If you've been calling your mom every day to talk about the break up, your mom is going to perpetuate the story you've been telling her: "What a horrible guy. He cheated!" Your mom is just going to help you with that story and recreate it every single day and every time you talk about it with her. It might feel good for a minute to talk through it and vent, but you're still re-experiencing the emotion over and over again with a negative energy attached.

Rather than relying on rehashing how and why the break up happened a million ways with your mother, focus on healing by calling someone who is going to help you get through your emotions. This person should ask you: "How are you feeling today?" and try to help you change your perspective regarding this event. A good advisor in this situation should ask if you can receive gratitude from this situation or see the bright side. They should help you think differently about the situation as you move forward. Someone willing to guide you with productive conversation could be a therapist, a coach, a mentor, your best friend, or your mother—anyone who is going to help empower the healing process instead of giving into gossip or perpetuating a venting spiral. People either keep you stuck in your negativity or help forge a path out of it.

The meaning we give every situation creates our experience of it. So is there a rationale for why this happened that is enlightening? Is there a possible reason the universe would want this person out of your life? Find the meaning that serves your healing, and you will find yourself with peace of mind sooner than later.

How do we know it's time to assess our wounds and heal?

When you begin your path toward personal growth and development, you become more and more aware of who you are and the characteristics that make you who <u>you are</u>—your frustrations, what makes you happy, what makes you proud, what makes you sad, what you are good at, what you are bad at. You then seek to elevate yourself to be a better version of yourself. When you're at that level, that's when you're ready to face your wounds and heal them. I advise my students and friends to "look at it"—look at the emotion and then let yourself feel it to the fullest extent. The bravest thing you can do is to look in the mirror and face yourself. What am I holding onto?

I currently have an amazing student in my Millionaire Program. While she was already quite successful, she signed up because she wanted to create more success in her life. During one of our classes, she got emotional and spoke up for the first time, stating that she realized that what she truly wanted was *to heal*. In all her years building toward success, she was never truly happy with any of it. The money, the cars, the cottage—none of it was making her truly happy. She realized that while she was on this path of growth and development, it was now her time to pause and heal.

I define my Millionaire Program—a personal development and growth program—as "spirituality meets personal growth and development." While the program centers on the energetics of wealth and success and growing your business, it is all framed as a healing process. I believe that in order for you to step into the millionaire version of yourself and grow, it requires self-awareness and healing. The program is less about having a million dollars in your account and more about being a millionaire in self-identity. You know that saying "I feel like a million bucks"? Well, what does that feel like? To me, this means peace of mind, joy, gratitude, fulfillment, love, freedom, ease, and flow. I want you to experience all of that whether you have a million dollars in your bank account or not. Then when the money comes, it's a bonus and you are fulfilled by all the universe has for you.

It's important to discern when to let certain people take part in your healing process. Not only can the process make us sensitive to the energies of those around us, but it can make us susceptible to our own negative projections. Remember, everything outside of you in the physical world is a reflection of what's going on inside you. Your outside world is your consciousness projected outward. Whatever you are seeing outside yourself is coming from within you. With this in mind, when we have haters coming at us, that means we have hate coming from within ourselves. Could this be projected from a past version of ourselves? Yes, but ultimately, that energy is coming from you directly in the present.

I recognize and take responsibility for all the contrast that has shown up in my life. I truly do believe that every effect is a direct cause of my own consciousness, not just the good manifestations but all of them. So instead of judging others, making them wrong and asking questions like, "Why is this happening to me," I ask instead, "How have I asked for this?" What in my thinking led me to this outcome? The beautiful thing is we have the ability to revise our manifestations, to switch their direction, and to select again, so asking these questions will help you do so. Essentially, this contrast has been awareness and shown me the path to be taken instead. What beautiful feedback, and powerful proof of my power.

So when you find yourself in conflict with people in your life, I would reflect on these questions. Is the other person in the wrong? Are they really against me? Is this happening on purpose and intentionally? Could my interpretation of the situation be changed? Am I really seeing what happened in a neutral way? The key to healing is being able to step back from the situation, gain neutrality, and ask the question: Is it possible that I'm wrong about this situation? That my perception isn't reflecting reality?

In the same vein, sometimes haters simply hate themselves more than they love themselves. Oftentimes, they are just projecting their own insecurities or mirroring your own insecurities back at you. If someone is being mean or cruel toward me, I now see that there's something within them that they're unhappy about that they're projecting onto me. The old Kathleen would have taken such behaviors to heart. The new Kathleen knows to step into grace and compassion. She lets her purpose take over. Now, every time it appears someone is cruel toward me, it makes me want to help them because everyone deserves to heal and become the best of themselves. I am also aware that everything is a reflection of something within myself. My consciousness has asked for this. Maybe I didn't think I deserved better? Maybe I'm used to people being this way to me? Maybe I don't think I'm worthy of better treatment? How can I turn to love more and be open to receive more love?

To start healing today, here is some advice for doing it on your terms. Hire a mentor, therapist, or coach to help you process your feelings in a productive way. Get into the practice of emotional journaling. Have a pad and paper by you at all times and notice your emotions throughout the day and record them. Simply ask: What is the emotion I'm feeling right now, and why am I feeling it? After you make this routine, you'll start to notice trends and patterns. Emotional regulation is a skill. To be able to become aware of, heal from, and change an emotional state takes practice. A guided thoughtwork session might be just the thing to help you.

Remember: Feel the feeling to heal the feeling!

CHAPTER 16:
Journal Prompts

Exploring the power of a healing support system: Reflect on the statement, "Sometimes we need an outside perspective when we need to heal out of a feeling." Consider instances when seeking support from others has played a role in your healing journey. How has the presence of a supportive and empathetic individual impacted your ability to heal and overcome challenges? Reflect on the qualities you value in a healing support system. What attributes or characteristics would you seek in someone who can promote your healing and growth? How can you actively cultivate a network of individuals who uplift and empower you on your path to healing?

Assessing the influence of external perspectives: Reflect on the statement, "You're going to want to make sure it's someone who is going to promote your healing instead of perpetuating the same story of suffering you're already stuck in." Explore the impact of external perspectives on your healing process. How have negative or unsupportive influences hindered your progress in the past? Reflect on the importance of surrounding yourself with individuals who uplift and encourage your healing journey. What steps can you take to minimize exposure to toxic or unsupportive influences and create boundaries that protect your well-being? How can you actively seek relationships and connections promoting healing and growth?

Empowering your healing journey: Consider the role of personal empowerment in your healing process. Reflect on the statement, "Sometimes we need an outside perspective when we need to heal out of a feeling." How can you harness your own inner strength and resilience to promote healing from within? Explore self-empowering practices such as self-reflection, self-care, and self-compassion. How can you cultivate a mindset that encourages self-healing and growth? Reflect on the ways in which you can take ownership of your healing journey and become an active participant in your own transformation. What empowering beliefs and affirmations can you incorporate daily to promote healing and positive change?

CHAPTER **SEVENTEEN:**

Self Definition

*Every decision that you make every second is not a decision about what to do;
it is a decision about who you are. Every act is an act of self-definition.*
-Neale Donald Walsch

The quote above is monumental in understanding why *now* is the time to choose to become the best of yourself. Everything we do, every single day, defines who we are in that moment and who we will continue to be. How you act today defines the next moment and influences your cause and your effect. How you respond to the world around you—other people and their behavior, crises, anything—reflects who you are and how you define yourself within the world. Every response counts, especially when life is caught in the ups and downs of its rhythm.

The best moments for self-definition happen in the moments where things aren't going just as we'd hoped. For this reason, I lean into the law of polarity, also known as the law of opposites. There are always two ends to every spectrum, up and down, high and low, near and far. So, this understanding helps to give perspective to why life will always have good things happen, as well as what we perceive as bad. I like to use the word *contrast* in this case. Contrast is when your experiences within the world run contrary to what you desire. For example, you say you want happiness but a sad thing happens, or you say you want more money, but instead, you go into debt or an unexpected bill comes.. The real reason for contrast and why it's so purposeful is because it gives you the opportunity to actually put the best of yourself into practice.

It's easy to be the best of yourself when there is no challenge or immediate obstacle. However, without contrast, are you really being the best of yourself? Or are you functioning on autopilot? Without any turbulence or opportunity to react to the outside world, we remain the same. Redefining yourself requires a response in moments of contrast. It means taking action, and usually new action.

My entire life before my awakening, I pushed for change to start on Monday. I would bargain with myself: "I'll eat healthy on Monday. I'll walk on Monday. I'll get started on Monday." I was constantly self-defining in that moment, solidifying that I was the kind of person who doesn't take action and instead procrastinates. I lacked discipline in parts of my life and failed to follow through on my own commands. I didn't realize that there is only one moment and one time to become the best of yourself, and that's right now. The present moment is an opportunity to define who you are and who you'll continue to be by the actions you take from the feelings you're in and the thoughts you have.

THERE IS ONLY
one moment
AND ONE TIME
TO BECOME
THE BEST OF
yourself,
AND THAT'S
RIGHT NOW.

The law of expression is something I always like to remind myself of. This law is always in place and it states that you express life based upon what you think of yourself, what you think of others, what you think of the world, and what you think that others think of you. You express life through your consciousness, in the moment. The law of expression also works in tandem with cause and effect because if life is a result of your consciousness, it is done so in a series of steps that are taken in a feeling and emotional conception of self, who you think yourself to be. If you want to change and become the best of yourself, recognize that now is THE time to start choosing to be the version of yourself. After all, you don't change your life in the *becoming*. You change your life in the *being*. There's a massive difference between the two. You are always expressing life through your consciousness lens, so if you change the lens, you change the expression. The world responds very differently as you respond differently to it.

One of my students took part in our Millionaire Program before attending our Miami retreat. She did all the self-image work, answered all the questions, and embodied all the lessons. When she participated in our guided visualization, she had an epiphany: *I am her.* She realized that she already was the best of herself. This whole time she was trying to be the best of herself, she didn't realize or conceive that she was already embodying that person. In that moment, she had a shift in her belief and her entire world changed. Everything around her became different. She's now in a completely different version of herself. She sees life differently, she's happy, she's grateful, she loves herself, and she behaves and expresses life from a completely different consciousness because she realized all she needed to do was <u>be</u> this version, not <u>become</u> it.

How can you be the elevated version of yourself starting today? In what way? Even when running errands, how can you go about this activity as the elevated version of yourself? When you go live on Instagram to talk about the business you are launching, who are you going to be? Who are you going to show up as when you go on that first date? To me, it's a conscious decision to <u>be</u> rather than to wait to be.

When I was choosing to put off change for Mondays, I was choosing and accepting an identity of myself that never follows through and leaves tasks for the future. It was deeply rooted in my identity. I habitually behaved that way, and it became my default setting. I was in a state of fear so I operated as such.

I honestly believe that the old Kathleen was scared. If I began elevating and choosing to change immediately, that meant I would start exercising and eating healthy and get skinny and become more visible. Our society sees bigger bodies as a flaw, but I no longer do. Still, at the time, I used the "flaw" of my bigger body as something to hide behind. I was worried that if I lost this flaw, I would become visible and thus susceptible to being judged as the entire package of Kathleen instead of just for the weight. For some people, a similar issue occurs when they believe they are imposters in their career or in their lives. What if we chose to become more visible? Not physically but for who we really are? I am becoming the best of myself every single day, and she is being seen honestly, boldly, and unapologetically. It can feel scary, but oh it feels so good.

As I understand it, imposter syndrome comes down to a lack of awareness. You believe that you aren't who you're trying to be. It resembles sitting in a boardroom with a bunch of execs. While you're at that table and have the title, you still feel as though you don't belong there. No one in that room is telling you that you don't belong—you are telling yourself that you don't belong. Essentially, you haven't accepted the identity that you are a high-level executive sitting at that table. This is a lack of awareness of realness for all that you are. You can't see what is already there. Many use the language, "Act as if," but I have found it limiting. I don't want to "act" as if I belong. I want to practice belonging. Practicing "being" the best of yourself is the key. One feels like pretending while another feels like existing as.

The world RESPONDS VERY DIFFERENTLY *as you respond* DIFFERENTLY TO IT.

Let's say you were asked to give a presentation on stage and teach 10,000 people. You're about to go up, but you don't think you're good enough. You don't believe you're worthy. You don't imagine you have enough to say. It's one thing to be nervous; it's another issue to feel like a fraud and sabotage yourself. To overcome this programming means you have to reconnect with the best of yourself.

When my clients experience something similar, I ask them to think of a situation in their life they are proud about and list the specifics, considering: What roles do I feel proud of?

Most of the time, impostor syndrome stems from a lack of worthiness. Do you feel worthy as a mother? As a child? As a leader? What roles do you feel worthy in? How can I grab that worthy feeling and inject it into this newer experience? It's not anything in your outside world that's telling you you're not good enough; it's your internal landscape informing yourself that you're not good enough. You're only peering through the lens of your limitation. The most straightforward solution is to change the lens and remove the limitation. What if we do not believe in imposter syndrome? I feel like it's simply a part of growth to not always feel like you belong as you rise in awareness levels, as you gain comfort. But the more you control your thinking, the more you convince yourself you do belong. Those you once looked up to become peers, first in your mind then in the physical.

In my Laws Course, I talk about the law of expression, as I believe we express life based on the beliefs we hold in our subconscious mind and patterns. We express life based on who we think we are, and what we think about ourselves. One of our beliefs could be that we're a fraud. We express life quite differently if we think we're frauds versus if we believe that we're meant to be there or if we're the best in our industry. If you think you're the best speaker in the world instead of thinking you're a fraud you're going to approach that stage and express yourself in two entirely different ways and create two different experiences. The response will obviously be different. You cannot move through this life without a consciousness tied to a subsequent expression. We behave based on who we think we are. So don't just try to change the behavior, but the underlying beliefs and the behavior change naturally.

Some people practice public speaking until they feel they've perfected it. They then wait for another person to say they're good before they go out and speak. We don't need to do that. You can actually create within yourself the belief that you're amazing, that you're good enough, and that the rest of the world will see that—that's the law. The law of expression says that based on what we think, feel, and express, the results in our life are formulated.

You get to decide the story and how it'll be expressed. You get to create the belief in the self, which will either propel you forward or hold you back. How we think and how we express these thoughts and feelings is our reality; luckily, we have the power to change it.

To remove certain limitations, first review our past chapters on taking things personally and healing. Here are a few ways you can practice embodying a limitless you on your own:

- Use self-suggestion to affirm a new narrative, one where you tell yourself all the ways that you're worthy, capable and courageous.

- Write yourself love notes and keep them by the bed. I write positive affirmations and love notes to myself when I stay in hotels on the little note pads next to the bed.

- Try journaling. Observe when and how the feelings come up and get to the root cause and narrative you're telling yourself. What is the underlying belief there?

- Do mirror work. Louise Hay was a profound innovator with this. Stand in front of the mirror, look yourself in the eye and give yourself love.

- Self-define your identity in that exact moment. The old you is afraid of X, Y, Z, but the new you is not the kind of person to hold back due to fear. *Be* that new you.

- Be clear on who you are being. Saying, "I am someone who…" has been profound for me. For example, saying, "I am someone who walks every day," has led my body to follow that very belief.

- Move out of judgment and into gratitude. Find things in your life to be grateful for, about yourself, about others, about this world. Drop any judgments.

- Enter into a state of love. Have grace and compassion for yourself. You'll make better decisions and attract better outcomes in a state of love versus a state of fear.

- Move into faith. Choosing to give it to god or the universe allows you to fully surrender to this new one, the one who is divinely created, guided, and supported.

During my classes, students often note how confidence manifests on the calls, namely, how it's a trait that many people want more of and think they don't have enough of. Now, it's one thing to make it an affirmation and say that you're confident, but it's another thing to act with confidence. It's about showing up and making the decision to act confidently, to be bold, to be loving and caring. This defines who you will become based on your actions and your decisions, which alter your outside world.

In relationships, so many people have fights, which I think is just a breakdown in confidence when one or both people lack the confidence to be honest about their feelings or their experience. Fights are disagreements between people, and acting in a state of confidence would mean that you and your partner are using that space to grow and work through your conflict rather than hold that space as a place for deterioration. When we're not acting confidently, we get our egos hurt in these spaces and aim to be hurtful rather than curious or gracious. Rather than the "yell, hurt each other, and then don't talk for two days" model, I want to understand why I'm reacting the way I'm reacting. I want to pay attention to my emotions and what's coming up for me and resolve our issues together. This comes from having confidence because I understand that every act is an act of self-definition. I could use this opportunity to grow and heal with someone, or to scream and fight instead. Overall, it takes confidence to do the more vulnerable maneuver and connect with someone.

In business, we have to remember nothing is personal. Business is professional and professionalism is a way of managing yourself while still holding space and managing other people's emotions. It's important to remember that other people's behaviors and actions in this space are not personal when it's a business decision. When someone decides to quit their job working for you, they are quitting their job to better their life in some way: money, commute, and title. Being confident and secure means that you can't believe that they are quitting you. You have to believe and define yourself as the kind of person who believes the right people will be working with you at the right moment. If someone is leaving your business, it's to make room for someone else to enter that's going to take you to the next level.

You're here because you have a burning desire to change. If you don't have a burning desire to change, nothing <u>will</u> change. I want you to take a moment and return to the initial reason why you picked up this book. Why do you want to become the best of yourself? Why put forth all that work? Solidify your reason and read this book again. I'm sure you'll see it in a whole new way.

Most importantly, I want you to know that you can start being the best of yourself right now in this very moment. You can choose to define yourself as being the best right now.

So what are you waiting for? Make the promise, the choice, and decision now. You'll be forever grateful that you did. How you show up today at this moment will determine what will show up for you tomorrow. My daughters loved the movie *The Greatest Showman*, and one line in a song from the soundtrack says "tomorrow starts tonight," and it's something I truly believe sets the successful apart and the best of yourself from the rest.

Every act
IS AN ACT
OF SELF-
definition.

CHAPTER 17:
Journal Prompts

Reflecting on the power of decision-making: Consider the statement, "Every decision you make—every decision that you make every second—is not a decision about what to do; it is a decision about who you are." Reflect on your choices and actions profoundly shaping your identity and defining yourself. Explore the idea that every decision, no matter how small, contributes to the overall narrative of your life. Take a moment to reflect on recent decisions you have made. How have they contributed to your self-definition? How can you make more conscious choices that align with the best version of yourself?

Embracing the opportunity for self-transformation: Reflect on the significance of the present moment and why now is the perfect time to choose to become the best version of yourself. Consider the statement, "Everything we do, every single day, defines who we are in that moment and who we will continue to be." Contemplate the idea that each day brings new opportunities for growth and self-improvement. How can you harness the power of the present moment to make choices that align with your values and aspirations? Reflect on the areas of your life where you desire personal growth and transformation. What steps can you take today to move closer to becoming the best version of yourself?

The impact of your responses on self-definition: Explore the concept that how you respond to the world around you reflects who you are and how you define yourself within the world. Reflect on the statement, "Every response counts, especially when your life becomes demanding or difficult." Consider recent challenging situations or interactions where your responses influenced your self-perception. How did you define yourself in those moments? Were there any responses that you would like to change or improve upon? Reflect on the power of conscious response in shaping your self-image and personal growth. How can you cultivate mindfulness and intentionality in your responses to positively impact your self-definition?

IN CONCLUSION

There are so many things I hope you have come to realize while reading this book. Who you believed you were when you started this book and who you believe you are at this moment are likely two different versions of you.

When I first started my journey of self-awareness, I believed I was flawed, I was a problem needing fixing, and I would forever be "less than" everyone else. It's like I wore this badge that said I was not pretty enough, not thin enough, not sexy enough. You name it, I thought it. But something magical happened when I started to question why.

Why do I think I am less than others?

Why do I believe I am flawed?

What makes me broken?

Whose beliefs are these?

Whose thoughts are these?

Did they really originate from within?

I hope you see that you have been divinely created, that your uniqueness is your superpower, that any way you see yourself as inferior isn't real but an illusion you believed. When you believed it, you made it so, and you continue to make it so by simply accepting it. The greatest freedoms I've ever encountered were ones done in my own thinking. It's like I had the key to my prison door in my pocket the whole time. When I dismissed my flaws once and for all, magic happened.

During one of my most recent live events, one of my students shared her quantum leap story, and she said so powerfully: "The moment I started loving myself is the moment the money started to come." This is a very important comment. It speaks to freedom, first in the mind, and then in the physical form. We attract "less than" experiences in our life: less money than we want, less love in our lives, less freedom because we believe we are less. Our worthiness determines the reality we experience. The moment you decide you are worthy, you become that. When you accept that you are more than average, that you are a bright light, the universe responds with "yes." Here is more love, here is more money, here is more freedom, because YES, you are worthy.

Someone asked me once, "How did you decide to just be okay with your flaw?" It felt almost like they were asking me how I decided to just accept my flaw in a "it is what it is" sort of way. But that's not what I did. Being fat was never wrong—my belief that it is/was wrong is the problem. Change the belief and change the experience. When I decided to see my curves as an asset, as beautiful, as what made me unique, the flaw disappeared. Remove the judgment. Even as you read this, you have been hardwired to think, "But it is unhealthy." I thought that too. I experienced years of guilt and shame for being an unhealthy and lazy member of society, when the reality was that I was healthier than many thin people. It's not a truth but a belief we accept as true over time. I am happy, healthy, and wealthy. This little sentence changed it all for me. Yes, I am curvier. Yes, I am healthy. Yes, I love myself.

This book is about freedom, about fulfillment, about joy, about love, and about peace of mind. It's the realization that all those things exist within you when you stop resisting them. The key is YOU. You were never made to try to be different. You were meant to be who you really are: yourself. What a magical idea.

I hope you see this as a returning home to the worthy and whole person you've always been. Welcome home to the best of yourself.

RESOURCES

**Stay connected with my energy to unlock your true potential!
Explore these incredible resources that promise
to inspire and uplift you.**

House of Manifestation - https://www.houseofmanifestation.com/

Diamond Academy - https://kathleencameronofficial.com/

Podcast - https://podcasts.apple.com/us/podcast/the-manifested-podcast-with-kathleen-cameron/id1649870563

YouTube - https://www.youtube.com/channel/UCjsVtfQBbHwfybcLIcnxEMA

SCAN HERE TO LEARN MORE ABOUT MY COMMUNITY!

WORKS CITED

"7 Levels of Consciousness." *7 Levels of Consciousness*, www.barrettacademy. com/7-levels-of-consciousness. Accessed 7 Aug. 2023.

Gallagher, Sandy. "Understanding the Seven Levels of Awareness." *Proctor Gallagher*, 10 June 2022, www.proctorgallagherinstitute.com/54261/ understanding-the-seven-levels-of-awareness.

Goddard, Neville. *The Power of Awareness*. Merchant Books, 2012.

Russell, Robert A. *God Works Through Faith*. Sanage Publishing House, 2023, pp 3. Print.

Singer, Michael A. *Living Untethered: Beyond the Human Predicament*. New Harbinger Publications, 2022.

Solomon, Robert C. *Existentialism*. 2nd ed. New York: Modern Library, 2005. Print.

Sullivan, Dan, and Benjamin Hardy. *The Gap and the Gain: The High Achievers' Guide to Happiness, Confidence, and Success*. Hay House, Inc., 2021.

Troward, Thomas. *The Dore Lectures on Mental Science*. Wilder Publications, 2018. Print.